THE OFFICIAL
STAR TREK
THE NEXT GENERATION
MAKEUP FX JOURNAL

Michael Westmore and Joe Nazzaro

"...it appears that I'll be spending the next several years going where no makeup artist has gone before..."
— MICHAEL WESTMORE

TITAN BOOKS

Contents

Produced by Starlog Communications International, Inc. for Titan Books Ltd

Editor
David Hutchinson

Managing Editor
Michael Benson

Contributing Editors
David McDonnell
Michael McAvennie
Anthony Timpone
Michael Gingold
Maureen McTigue
Lia Pelosi

Art Director
Calvin Lee

Art Staff
Jim McLernon
Yvonne Jang
Len H. Leake
Susan Sung

Production Staff
Steve Jacobs
Paul Hallasy

Contributors
Cliff Bole, LeVar Burton, Michael Dorn, Jonathan Frakes, Brent Spiner, Les Landau, Andy Probert, Majel Barrett Roddenberry, Rick Sternbach, Patrick Stewart, Michael Westmore Jr.

Dedication
TO MY CHILDREN:
Michael, Michele and McKenzie, and my wife Marion, who is my love and guiding light.
— *Michael*

TO SHEELAGH:
I hope our partnership never ends. — *Joe*

Acknowledgment
Without an outstanding makeup and hairstyling crew, the special visual quality of *Star Trek* would not be possible. I applaud and commend my staff for all their long hours and their makeup artistry. I wish to express special thanks to makeup artists Gerald Quist, June Haymore, Jana Phillips, Jill Rockow, Craig Reardon, Doug Drexler, Edward French, Werner Keppler, and hair stylists Richard Sabre, Vivian McAteer, Yolanda Toussieng, Susan Carol-Schwary, Candy Neal, Joy Zapata and many, many more.
— *Michael Westmore*

THE OFFICIAL STAR TREK THE NEXT GENERATION MAKEUP FX JOURNAL
ISBN 1 85286 491 5

Published by Titan Books Ltd, 42-44 Dolben Street, London SE1 0UP

First Titan edition November 1993
10 9 8 7 6 5 4 3 2 1

British Library Cataloguing-in-Publication Data. A catalogue record for this book is available from the British Library.

Printed and bound in Great Britain by Stephens and George Ltd, Merthyr Industrial Estate, Dowlais, Merthyr Tydfil.

For a complete list of Star Trek publications, please send a large stamped SAE to Titan Books Mail Order, 42-44 Dolben Street, London SE1 0UP. Please quote reference NGMUJ on both envelopes.

Introduction

By BRENT SPINER

If I had to name one single element that has been responsible for the success of *STAR TREK: THE NEXT GENERATION,* I would say it's Michael Westmore. There have been times where we haven't had a great script, or our performances haven't been very memorable, but I can't remember a time when Michael's work hasn't been great. It's been the grounding for the whole show, and I think without him, *THE NEXT GENERATION* would never have become the success it has.

The process of putting on makeup every day is a tedious one from the moment you start in the morning until the end of the day. It's a given that my eyes are going to hurt all the time, and by the middle of the day, there's going to be makeup in my eyes along with the contacts. There is just nothing pleasant about it, other than the fact that Michael is such an enjoyable person to spend time with. If I didn't like Michael as much as I do, I would find it intolerable. I always know that when I arrive in the morning, as tired as I may be, or as much as I don't want to sit there and have makeup put on, I am going to have a nice conversation with Michael, and it's going to be a pleasant hour and 15 minutes.

When I had to play the character of Dr. Soong in "Brothers," I didn't have a clue as to who the character was. He was just a generic old man. It wasn't until I saw the makeup on my face that I knew what to do. At least 75 percent of that performance was due to Michael, because the makeup told me who the character was. He put the idea onto my face, and I suddenly understood too. It was an enormous help.

I've never experienced a situation where Michael has dried up

in terms of ideas. He gets handed a script that says "alien," and the next thing you know, Michael has invented some wonderful creature that elevates the show artistically.

I suspect that the success or failure of *DEEP SPACE NINE* also rests in the hands of Michael Westmore. I have nothing but high hopes for the show, because if it's a project where Michael is doing the makeup, it can't help but be a success. There is a consistency and a brilliance to his work that cannot be found anywhere else. ●

Beginnings

Westmore pauses with Ferengi friend.

The road to *STAR TREK: THE NEXT GENERATION* started almost 30 years ago for me. When I started working as a makeup artist in 1961, I never would have dreamed that someday I would be working on a TV series that would challenge and excite me the way *THE NEXT GENERATION* does on a weekly basis.

I come from a long line of makeup artists, starting with my grandfather George Westmore, who founded the first studio makeup department in 1917. A generation later, each of the six Westmore brothers became a successful makeup artist in his own right. My father Mont was head of makeup at Selznick-International, working on films such as

Rebecca and *Gone With the Wind*. Perc was in charge of makeup at Warner Bros., and worked with stars like Bette Davis, Errol Flynn and Paul Muni, who thanked him during his acceptance speech for the Best Actor Oscar in 1936.

Ern was head of makeup at RKO and later, 20th Century Fox, and counted John Barrymore and W.C. Fields as his confidantes. He also created the look for actresses Katharine Hepburn and Claudette Colbert. Wally headed the makeup department at Paramount, where stars like Bing Crosby, Bob Hope and Ray Milland were close companions. His makeup for Fredric March in *Dr. Jekyll and Mr. Hyde* helped the actor win an Oscar in 1931.

Frank was head of makeup on

The Ten Commandments, and Bud is probably best known for creating *The Creature from the Black Lagoon* while supervising the makeup at Universal.

It was my Uncle Bud who gave me the chance to become a makeup artist in 1961. Bud had become almost a surrogate father to me, and I used to go over to his house to swim in the pool, do some work in his wood shop, and maybe stay for dinner. Because of my mother's insistence and Bud's fondness for me, I was offered an apprenticeship at Universal.

During my first few months as an apprentice, my main responsibilities were ordering supplies, doing paperwork and getting coffee. In the morning, I had to be available if anyone in the department needed something, but I wasn't actually allowed to do any makeup. If I wanted to practice, I would have to grab a secretary or a makeup artist who wasn't doing anything.

In the afternoons, I would learn the techniques of makeup. I spent six months learning how to do beauty makeup, then six months learning how to lay a beard, apply a bald cap and so forth. While this was going on, makeup artist John Chambers came over to Universal from NBC, and I spent a lot of time with him working in the lab. It was John who gave me most of my lab background and taught me how to be self-sufficient on a project.

After finishing my apprenticeship, I stayed with Universal until 1971. In 1965, I was made assistant department head, and because John Chambers left the studio to do *Planet of the Apes,* I had to run the lab as well. During that period of time, I was involved with every Universal film that included appliance work.

In 1971, I decided to leave Universal to become a freelance makeup artist. I happened to run into Sid and Marty Kroft, who were starting up some new shows, and they offered me the chance to become the appliance makeup artist for their company. During that period, I worked on shows like *Sigmund and the Sea Monsters, The New Zoo Revue,* and *The Land of the Lost,* for which I received an Emmy nomination in 1976.

Around that time, I was also in business with my brother Marvin, instructing plastic surgeons in the use of therapeutic cosmetic aids. Marvin and I would alternate films, while the other person ran the shop. In the mid-70s, I was offered a small, low budget film which turned out to be *Rocky,* and that started my career rolling in feature films. After *Rocky,* director Peter Hyams offered me *Capricorn One,* Martin Scorsese asked me to do *Raging Bull,* and it went on from there.

Rocky was an important film for me, not only because it won the Academy Award for Best Picture that year, but also because of the amount of work I did on it. I was the only makeup artist on the film, and during the fight sequences, I had to run back and forth between Sylvester Stallone and Carl Weathers, changing their makeups. I would switch the appliances around the upper and lower eyes, the cheeks and the rest of the face, which continued to swell as the fight went on.

My experiences on *Rocky* held me in good stead when I started *Raging Bull,* which I worked on steadily for 14 months. Robert DeNiro had different appliances on his face for every single scene in the film, including different nose styles, cuts, bruises and stitches, and a vast number of facial appliances needed for the fight sequences. It was a tremendously demanding film, working

Westmore applies *2010* makeup to Dullea

with two perfectionists like Scorsese and DeNiro, but it was rewarding as well. When DeNiro won the Best Actor Oscar that year, I was the second makeup artist to be thanked by an actor at the Academy Awards.

If I had to pick some of the other high points from my film career, the three that come to mind would be *Mask, 2010* and *Clan of the Cave Bear. Mask* is an obvious choice, because it earned me an Oscar in 1986. They talked to virtually every appliance makeup artist in Hollywood before offering me a job, and I spent three months doing makeup tests to see how my design would look on film. I created eight different heads before we decided on the final makeup, which had to be cast from a thick, heavy rubber to simulate the bone growth of the disease. The final design worked very well, as evidenced by the public's response to the film.

With *2010,* I had a significant restriction to work with, because Keir Dullea's old age makeup had to look similar to his previous appearance in *2001.* There was literally no still photography done on the earlier movie, so the studio had to blow up individual frames of film so I would have something to copy.

From what I understand, Keir's makeup in the original film took almost 11 hours to apply. He was dreading the thought of having to go through it again, but I had two other makeup artists, including my brother Monty, and a hairstylist working with me, and

The finished *2010* makeup.

Michael Westmore displays some of his makeup "trophies."

into a great looking 10-minute segment. If the film had sound on it, I think it might have gotten nominated, but it only got as far as the final seven. It was probably the longest 10 minutes of my life, sitting there with no sound.

Although I spent a good part of my time on film, there were also a number of television projects of which I'm very proud. As of this writing I have just received my 24th Emmy nomination. Among the high points would be *Eleanor*

Westmore received an Oscar for his *Mask* makeup.

we were able to cut it down to five-and-a-half hours. Keir actually does a lot of yoga, so while we were doing his makeup, he would do his meditation, and when we were finished, he would get up from the chair as spry as when he first sat down.

One morning, after Keir had been made up, the two of us were walking down the street together, when a man pulled up next to us in a Jaguar. He looked at Keir and said, "Aren't you the old man from *2001*?" Keir smiled and nodded his head, and as we walked away, he looked at me and gave a little wink. I remember thinking to myself, "I guess we did a pretty good job!"

Working on *Clan of the Cave Bear* presented its own unique set of problems. There were 24 major actors on the film, and I had to make foreheads and teeth for each of them, as well as getting wigs made.

We had to start working very early each morning, and because we only had nine makeup artists on location, we had to make-up the actors in three waves that took two-and-a-half hours each. My main responsibility was the character of Creb, who had a stump at the end of one arm, and an eye socket that had been gouged out by a bear. There were

other effects that had to be created, such as one man whose head is ripped off during a fight with a cave bear and Daryl Hannah's leg swelling from an injury.

Because we were filming on a mountain top, the actors would stick the fake teeth in their pockets in-between shots, and every night, someone would sit on their teeth and break them. I would have to fix anywhere from one to six sets each day.

One film that never got the attention it deserved was *Masters of the Universe*, which didn't really find its audience until it was released on video. Because of budget restrictions, a lot of work I did on the film was never seen. I designed a mechanized, radio-controlled tail for one of the reptilian bounty hunters which was largely ignored, as was a little alien creature I made-up for a scene in Skeletor's chamber. The only way to really see him is by freeze-framing the tape.

Out of all the films I've done, I would have loved to win an Oscar for *Masters of the Universe*. In order to put a film up for nomination, you have to go to the Academy with 10 minutes of footage which is screened, but Cannon was going bankrupt at the time and couldn't give me any film with sound on it. They gave me a film with no sound to edit. My son Michael edited it together

and Franklin, which earned me my first Emmy in 1976, *Why Me*, a television movie with Glynis O'Connor that I'm very proud of, and *The Day After*, one of the most controversial projects I've ever worked on.

While I was working on *The Day After*, director Nicholas Meyer insisted that the makeup be as authentic as I could manage. The week before we started production, the army released all the motion picture footage it had shot in Hiroshima, showing the effects of radiation over a period of time. I made several pages of notes, charting the aftereffects of radiation poisoning, so that I was able to recreate the effects for television. Nicholas fought with ABC to maintain the authenticity of our work, and while parts of the film had to be cut, most of it did wind up on the small screen.

A friendly Benzite poses with the "creator."

My involvement with *STAR TREK: THE NEXT GENERATION* began in the late 1980s. After spending the last several years travelling around the world doing films, I had reached a point in my career where I wanted something that would keep me home a little more. I thought it was time to slow down, and yet I didn't want to do a half-hour sitcom or a one-hour soap opera. The kind of makeup I do is very creative, and you don't often find it on TV.

When *THE NEXT GENERATION* came along, it afforded me the chance to stay home and be creative on a steady basis. There's a new challenge every week, whether it's an old-age makeup, an alien, or an android that has to be opened up to reveal the electronics blinking away under its skin. I have done more work in five years of *THE NEXT GENERATION* than I have in my entire career, because of the the show's creative demands.

I wasn't actually called in when they first started interviewing makeup artists for the series, but when they asked several of my colleagues where they would go for lab work or appliances that had to be built, my name came up several times. It finally got to the point where the producers said, "Why don't we just call him and see if he's interested?" I was called into the studio on a Thursday, and met with Rick Berman and Bob Justman, who were the co-producers, and David Livingston, the production manager. We talked for about an hour. At that point, I had to leave, because I had an appointment with Whoopi Goldberg to make a small dental appliance for one of her acts. When I got home, there was a message on my answering machine saying I had the job if I wanted it. I called them back and said I was interested, but I wanted to think about it. Taking the job meant a long-term commitment; it meant I couldn't do feature films, and I would have to stay in the same place for several months, something I hadn't done in years.

The producers told me, "You don't have a lot of time to think about it, because we start doing our makeup tests on Monday," and this was Thursday. I literally had an hour to decide. My wife and I talked about it, and we both agreed that it would be a great opportunity. I called the producers back, and said, "OK, let's go," and that was it. We started doing makeup tests the following Monday, and I met the rest of the cast over the next several days. We were off and running.

My main responsibilities on the new series were to devise all the creatures and appliances, supervise the general makeup and maintain the show's overall look.

As far as the initial guidelines for the series, there weren't many restrictions as to what could be done with the makeup. We basically followed Gene Roddenberry's belief that as we travelled around the universe, we would encounter beings that would have some sort of human element, even if it's just a lower lip, a nose or their eyes. There always has to be a bit of humanity in them that the audience can relate to.

I found this approach to be more interesting, because each of our creations has a basis in reality. Whenever we started thinking about a new race of aliens, they had to have an element of humanity to them, and that's one of the reasons why the series has stayed popular for so many years. I am very proud of my makeup staff, for over the last five years we have been nominated for seven Emmys, having won the first season with the episode called "Conspiracy."

In the pages to follow, I'll be talking about some of the humanoid and alien races I've created for *STAR TREK: THE NEXT GENERATION,* and revealing for the first time, a few of our best kept makeup secrets. It gives me great pleasure to take you on this journey behind the scenes, and reintroduce you to some of my old friends. It should be fun. •

Androids & Electronics

The first major electronic makeup effect was in "Datalore"; Data's forehead was torn open, exposing his circuitry

Having an android as a main character in *THE NEXT GENERATION* has given me the unique opportunity to combine a lifetime of makeup experience with the cutting edge of modern technology. When we first introduced Data (played by Brent Spiner) in our pilot episode, I had no idea that over the next five years, we would find so many ingenious ways to show his inner workings. We've opened up parts of his positronic brain on several occasions, we've taken him apart a piece at a time, and on one occasion, placed his disembodied head on a shelf.

One of the reasons we've been able to create such convincing electronic FX is the help of my son, Michael Westmore Jr., who designs and builds the systems and circuits needed to achieve the proper illusions. If I come up with a new idea, I know Michael, Jr. can put it together—usually on very short notice. The fusion of makeup and technology is what makes Data such an interesting character, for us and our viewers.

When we first started testing Brent's makeup for Data, I didn't have a specific concept in mind for him. We worked for three or four days, trying every possible combination of hair and makeup you can imagine, until we found something that looked sufficiently "android-like."

Data's actual skin color is a very pale gold. I use an opalescent beige base into which I mix different colored powders to create a glow. Once the powders have been packed into the base, I pencil in his hairline.

Brent's makeup has literally not changed from day one. His face looks exactly the same as it did on the first day of filming. The skin will occasionally pick up a different tint if the surrounding objects throw color on it, but Marvin Rush does a wonderful job of lighting, and if you catch Data in a close-up, where he's lit by himself, you can see the gold skin color.

After we decided on the pale gold makeup, we went with a set of yellow contact lenses that complemented the look. It's a soft

Brent Spiner on Playing Data

"Tin Man" Photo by Robbie Robinson: ©1992 Paramount Pictures

Gene Roddenberry said to me at one point, "Would you be willing to change your appearance to play the role?" I said sure, because I was thinking ears, but since they had already done ears, I didn't know what they were going to come up with. Initially, they said, "Would you mind shaving your head for the part?" and I said, "I would mind that. If the show is going to run for six years, I don't want to have to shave my head every day for six years!" They said that could be a deal-breaker, because there was another guy being considered for the part, who didn't have hair. Then they came back and said, "What about changing the color of your skin?" I said fine, there would be no problem with that. They did 35 or so makeup tests with every color with every combination of skin, hair and eye color imaginable, and they finally settled on what you now see. It's the same makeup I wore on the very first day.

It was never spelled out to me that, "you will be sitting in makeup for an hour and 15 minutes every morning, you will be there before anyone else, you will be there for a minimum of 15 hours a day in that makeup, and you won't be able to touch your face, your costume or anyone else all day long." None of that was described. I'm not sure it would have made a difference, but I don't think you can ever know what this experience is like until you've done it.

—*Brent Spiner*

lens that Brent actually puts in himself and wears all day. He's worn them for so long that they've become almost second nature to him.

One of the consequences of having an android in a lead role was that I soon found myself creating various limbs and body parts for him in different episodes. For the first season story, "Datalore," the script called for Data to find an empty head mold used to create his brother Lore. The plastic shell was a vacuform taken from a head cast of Brent, which was also used to create the dummy head for Lore. I still have that head on a shelf in my lab.

In "The Measure of a Man," there was a scene where Riker has to remove one of Data's arms during a Starfleet hearing. Since they were going to be shooting close-ups of the arm, it had to be

painted the same color as the rest of Brent's makeup. There were no electronics involved, but I wanted the scene to look realistic.

There have been episodes where I've had to devise android effects which haven't been quite as serious. For "The Outrageous Okana," I built a pair of oversized teeth for Brent's encounter with the Comedian, played by Joe Piscopo. When Joe came in, he was wearing some Jerry Lewis teeth he used in his comedy routine, and Brent wanted a pair just like his for the scene where he tried to learn the meaning of comedy. It was a set of thin acrylic dentures that snapped on over the actor's real teeth.

The day we were filming the scene, Joe arrived at the studio at 7 a.m., and gave me his fake teeth, which had to be fixed. I re-

paired them and then made a quick copy for Brent, which I brought onto the set just as they were getting ready to rehearse.

A few weeks later, I had to make Data a fake beard for "The Schizoid Man." He was supposed to be copying Riker's beard, and since the scene was being played for humorous effect, I wanted to come up with something that wasn't perfect, as if Data had created it with one of the ship's replicators. I hand-laid the beard onto a rubber head, and then sprayed it to retain the proper shape. The color was blended to match Brent's hair, and the beard was transferred to his head in one piece.

Because we've done so many stories requiring android parts and limbs, I've had to make several casts of Brent's head and body over the last five years. The process can be uncomfortable for

Data sports
facial hair in
"The Schizoid Man."

Riker removes one of Data's arms
in "The Measure of a Man."

interesting to put something like a set of blinking lights on his head, so when he took off his VISOR, it would appear to be connected to them.

Michael, Jr. built a pair of little metal attachments that had a flat bottom that could be glued down, and a blinking LED mounted in it. A small wire ran through LeVar Burton's hair, down the back of his neck, and into a battery pack under his arm to make the devices blink.

Coincidentally, the little blinkers look exactly like the *Enterprise*. They have little fins coming out of the back, and the round pod up front is where the LED is mounted. I have three working pairs of blinkers: A fine pair for closeups, a medium pair and a heavy-duty pair that a stuntman could wear without damaging.

The electronic effects devised for Data started slowly at first. Michael, Jr. and I would throw in little bits to make a shot more interesting, but once the writers noticed what we were doing, they would write a script that would say, "Data opens up his arm," or, "They open up the side of Data's head." The effects became increasingly more complex, and we had a lot of fun trying to come up with new ideas that lent themselves to the stories.

Our first major electronic effect for Data was in "Datalore." After getting kicked in the head by Lore, a flap of skin on Data's forehead gets torn open, exposing the circuitry beneath. Michael, Jr. and I devised a means of combining prosthetics and circuitry to create a convincing illusion; a system we continued to improve on over the years. First, we pick an area we want to "open up," then I build a thin fiberglass shell that fits over it and a foam latex appliance that goes over the top of that. If the area runs into the hair, I lay hair over the appliance, and where it meets the skin, I paint it with Data's normal colors. Meanwhile, Michael, Jr. builds his electronics into the shell, and we glue the shell and the latex appliance together. The cords usually run through Brent's hair,

Unfortunately, I should have used more release agent, because when we went to take off the mold, his curly chest hairs had become imbedded in the alginate. I had to get a pair of long surgical shears, and little by little, each hair had to be cut away from the mold. By the time we got it off, he had a shaved chest! Brent was really nice about it, but he's never forgotten, and we've joked about it many times since then.

The first electronic effect that my son and I created wasn't for Data; it was actually the little blinkers that attach Geordi's VISOR to the sides of his head. The idea for the devices came out of a conversation Michael, Jr. and I had while walking across the parking lot to the production office. We thought it would be

some actors, but Brent has almost always been good natured about it. There was one occasion, however, that he has never let me forget. We had an episode in the first season where we had to open Data's chest, and I needed to make a cast of Brent's body to create the appliance. He laid on the floor, and after coating his chest with release agent, I smeared the alginate over the area we were casting.

and down his back to an off-camera control panel.

The success of our experiment in "Datalore" prompted us to try bigger and better effects in future stories. While it would be impossible to list everything we've done, there are a few episodes I really enjoyed. In terms of sheer size, I would have to pick "The Best of Both Worlds—Part II." There was a long sequence where Data is electronically hooked up to Picard, who has been transformed into a Borg. We had six different patterns of lights running at the same time, each of them blinking at random. Michael, Jr. hooked them up to a rheostat, which made them blink faster or slower.

The smallest effect we ever devised was for "Brothers," where Lore had to open up his thumb, revealing a teleportation device inside it. I had to make a cast of Brent's real thumb, and then build the fiber glass shell and the thin layer of rubber skin that covered it. Michael, Jr. devised the light boards and the controller, and hooked them to a nine-volt battery. The entire system was literally small enough to fit into the thumb area and a bit of the hand. We mounted the fake thumb on a grip stand, and shot it in extremely tight close-up, so it appeared that Brent was opening his own thumb.

There was another effect in "Brothers" that took a lot of work but turned out very well—that was the scene where Dr. Soong replaces one of Data's programming chips. Part of the neck had to open up, and a little probe comes out. The chip is placed on the probe, which then slides back into the neck. From a cast of Brent's head, we made a fake head into which Michael, Jr. built the electronics. We then glued a flap onto Brent's neck to match the flap on the mechanical head, and the camera cut back and forth between the two heads.

One of my other favorite episodes is "Q-Pid," a light-hearted story which contained some nice effects. We had one scene where Data opens up a flap in his arm, and a tremendous amount of light poured out of the electronic interior. Because of the way that sequence was shot, we had to find a way to design it around Brent's arm. Michael, Jr. found a new circuit board, material that was as thin as paper, and he built the blinking lights onto the board which was wrapped around Brent's wrist. I added an appliance which covered his arm, so when he flips open his wrist, it looks as

Creating Electronic FX

I started developing computer systems with a friend of mine as a hobby in high school, and I had done some little mechanical effects for my dad in other shows. There were new LEDs being made, and semi-conductors were coming down greatly in size, and I said to him, "What if we started building appliances with lights built into them?" The first thing we did was Geordi's blinkies, and it evolved into the story where Data meets up with Lore, and Lore kicks him in the head. That was the first major thing circuit-wise, and they kept getting more and more complex.

I'm currently building a couple of things for the new season, just to have them in stock. I've revamped the laser we did for Picard [Locutus], making it even smaller, and we're going to try to use that in something.

I'm also rebuilding all the controllers for when Data gets opened up and the lights start spinning around. I'm rebuilding them with microprocessors, so they're now the size of a beeper. They've got a little control pad on it, and all you have to do is tap a button, and you can tell it exactly what you want to do.

My dad and I have talked about building an alien out of transparent urethane, and putting fluorescent lights underneath the surface of the skin to give it a glow, like the fish people who had the fins on top of their heads. We've also talked about a few other ideas, such as attaching a laser to a servo so you can make it spin around with a remote control. Everything's coming down tremendously in size, and there are so many things we'll be able to do.

—*Michael Westmore, Jr.*

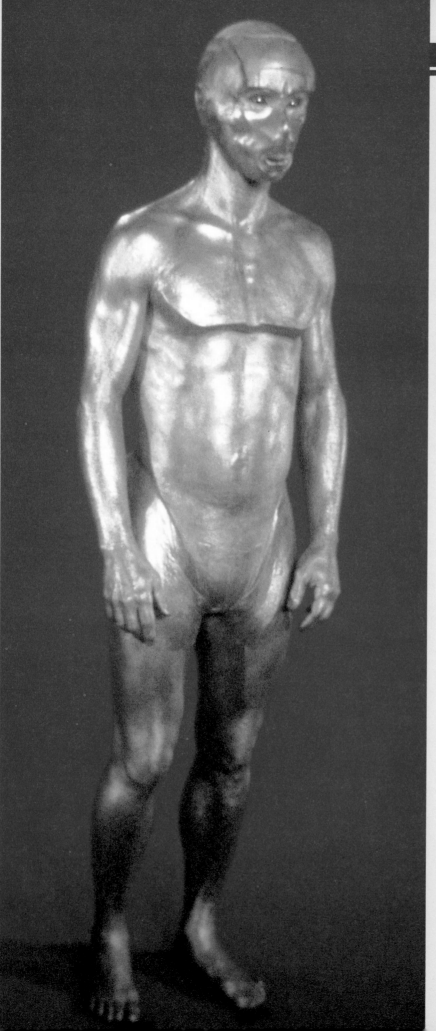

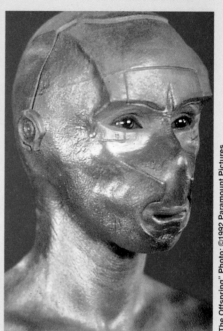

Leonard Crowfoot as Lal in "The Offspring" involved one of Michael Westmore's most memorable makeups.

if the light was coming out of him.

Another effect in "Q-Pid" that didn't get as much attention was Data's Friar Tuck makeup. Instead of placing his wig over a standard bald cap, we made an appliance for the top of his head that was segmented with different compartments that looked like they could be opened.

Several of our recent episodes have called for Data's head to be separated from his body for various reasons; in each case, we had to find a different method to approach the challenge. In "Disaster," Riker removes Data's still-sentient head and hooks it into the ship's computer. We didn't want the effect to look like a man sticking his head up through a table, so the scene was staged with Brent standing underneath a shelf. His body was optically removed in post-production, and we built a prosthetic collar at the base of Brent's neck to reinforce the idea that his head had been removed. Michael, Jr. built a row of blinking lights for the collar to make it look more interesting, and also to draw the viewers attention away from the space beneath the shelf. Brent had to keep his head perfectly still while the scene was being shot, so the appliance wouldn't buckle under the downward pressure.

In the first part of "Time's Arrow," the opening scene called for Data's head to be uncovered in a 19th-Century archaeological dig. I had to create two fake heads: One which was "antiqued," to appear as if it had been lying in a cave for several centuries, and a second, newer-looking head. A back panel was built into each head, which could be opened. In "Part II," where Geordi starts up Data's systems, Michael, Jr. built rows of lights into the sides and back of the head—the first time we had used two sets in conjunction.

Although we've created some amazing effects for Data in *THE NEXT GENERATION,* the most unforgettable work we've done with an android was in "The Offspring," which featured Lal, a being created by Data. If I had to list 10 of the most memorable makeups I've done in my career, this would be one of them.

One of the biggest reasons for the success of Lal's makeup was the amount of discomfort actor Leonard Crowfoot was willing to undergo for his three days of filming. Only one actor in a thousand would have agreed to endure what Leonard endured, and it was only with his help that we were able to create such an aggressive and complex makeup.

The script called for an androgynous-looking android, that would change its appearance later on in the episode. We wanted to give it a sexless appearance, so the first thing we did was change the appearance of Leonard's chest. We built a square pectoral chest covering that changed the roundness of his natural chest and did away with the nipples.

For Lal's head, we made a full head appliance that covered the nose and ears, and dropped the mouth area down to the chin. As a result, Leonard couldn't hear well, couldn't breath through his nose, and because he was wearing silverized contact lenses, his vision was severely impaired. In order to breath, he had to stick his finger in the mouth hole and open it up a bit in between scenes.

Two heads are better than one, as with Data's heads created for "Time's Arrow."

"Time's Arrow" Photo: Courtesy Michael Westmore

Director Les Landau on "Time's Arrow"

"I remember calling Michael when I read the first draft of 'Times Arrow', says director Les Landau, "and saying, 'There's a scene where Geordi is working on Data's head. It would be really neat to show all those inner workings. If you make it, I will film it.' Michael said he would come up with the device, and I think it was the first time we were able to show both the side and the back of Data's head simultaneously. I think it's something the audience likes to see, and it's also important to the story."

To top it all off, we built a giant foam appliance that covered Leonard's crotch area. He was glued into it every day, which meant that he couldn't go to the bathroom while he was wearing it. On the days that Leonard worked, he wouldn't eat or drink for the entire day, because it was a four-hour makeup in the morning, followed by 12 hours during the day, and it took almost two hours to get him out of it at night. We used a makeup called PAX, which literally sealed him into the appliances, and had to be scrubbed off with a loofa sponge. On the first night we cleaned Leonard up, one of our makeup artists, Doug Drexler, actually got in the shower with him to scrub him down. We kept coming up with different combinations of makeup remover, and by the final night, we were able to get him out of the makeup in an hour and 20 minutes, as opposed to two.

Once Lal had decided on its physical appearance, the role was taken over by Hallie Todd, who gave an innocent, Snow White type of look. We also had to create an elaborate electronic effect for the scene where Data touches her, and the top of her head opens up. I had to build a fiberglass skull structure with a matching wig section, and Michael, Jr. added the lights. We needed a tremendous amount of power for all the blinking lights, and we couldn't let them run for too long because of the heat.

That sequence blew everybody away. The camera was mounted a little higher than usual, and everybody was standing there, not knowing what to expect. Hallie's head appliance was attached to a piano wire, so when Data touches her on cue, I pulled the wire and the head opened up, revealing the blinking lights. It was a tremendously effective scene.

Looking ahead to future episodes, while it's too early to know what sort of electronic effects we'll be asked to create, Michael, Jr. and I already have several new ideas we're looking forward to trying out. It seems safe to assume that our most spectacular illusions are yet to come. ●

This is one of the first publicity stills of a Ferengi.

The Ferengi

The Ferengi crash a party on the *Enterprise* in "Menage a Troi."

The Ferengi, that annoying race of alien scavengers, were first seen in "The Last Outpost," one of our earliest episodes. My role in their development began when I was given a color rendering of the creatures by our senior illustrator, Andy Probert. His original concept was that the Ferengi had large pointed ears like a bat, so that they could hear sounds coming from any direction. His idea was interesting, but the producers thought the big ears would resemble oversized Vulcan ears, and asked me to round them off.

The drawing of the Ferengi also had a nose that was slightly different from our final version, as well as a long extended chin that made it look more like a witch than an alien. When I started sculpting the original head, the first thing I did was remove the points from the ears and make them rounder. I then did away with the chin, because it would have added more makeup time. I made a few other minor changes, and then finished the design by adding some more wrinkles across the bridge of the nose.

When the head was finished, I fashioned a small set of piranha-like teeth to fit into the actor's mouth. The final makeup consisted of a head piece with large ears, a nose appliance and upper teeth. I was quite satisfied with the finished product, which combined the best of Andy's ideas with my own modifications.

I was far less happy with a photo that surfaced soon after we finished filming "The Last Outpost," which showed one of our Ferengi actors without his pointed

The Ferengi made their debut in "The Last Outpost"; despite a few minor changes, their makeup has remained the same. from season to season.

A set of pointed lower teeth was added to the original design for the Ferengi's return appearance in "The Battle."

An unwitting Ferengi (Pater Shutsker) challenges Riker to a game of three-dimensional chess in "Menage a Troi."

In "The Price," a Ferengi delegation joins the negotiations for navigation rights to the Barzan Wormhole.

teeth. He was one of those happy-go-lucky kind of guys, and was probably standing on the street in his makeup when somebody asked him to mug for the camera. The next thing we knew, wham! That picture was everywhere!

I was annoyed about that photo because the makeup was incomplete. After all the work that went into it, we would have wanted our design in proper form. The photo was like a pirated version of our makeup, because none of us would have ever approved it under those circumstances.

In addition to the makeup appliances, a little symbol for each Ferengi was hand-painted onto the right lobe of their heads with a stencil. The design itself was created by scenic art supervisor/technical consultant Michael Okuda, and the little symbol he based it on actually means "Dog eat dog." We decided to paint it green for greed and the color of money. The entire design consists of the "Dog eat dog" preceded by a rocker.

If you look very closely at some of the Ferengi we've had in different episodes, you'll see that they have none, one, two or even three of those rocker symbols tattooed on their heads. The symbol without a rocker is the very lowest grade, then a single rocker, which denotes a second-grade Ferengi, a double rocker, which indicates a higher status, and a triple rocker, which is almost like a general. We've only seen a Ferengi triple rocker once or twice. Each Ferengi adds an additional mark as he goes up in power, although we're still not sure what happens if one of them is reduced in rank. I suppose we would have to create some kind of scar to show that a rocker has been removed.

When we brought back the Ferengi in "The Battle" a few episodes later, I added a set of lower teeth to my original design. Recalling their first appearance, we didn't think it looked right for them to have pointed teeth on top and straight teeth on the bottom. This time, I decided to add the bottom row as well.

Over the next few years, I continued to refine and improve the look of the Ferengi, trying to find subtle ways of making them evolve. During the second or third season, I added cheekbones to give their faces more development. Seeing these creatures with their oversized heads and big ears, I thought it was starting to look as if they were wearing masks. They also had smooth faces with no cheekbones, which didn't make them look especially mean and tough. By giving them the very exaggerated cheek bones, it gave the faces a much-needed angularity.

Another major improvement was the use of an airbrush, which helped me to add more color and shadow to the makeup. The original Ferengi were hand-painted their orangy skin color, but when I started to experiment with the airbrush, I discovered it was possible

to get better mottling and a lot more variable colors into the designs. Now, our Ferengi have more depth and contrast in their makeup than the earlier ones.

I also continued to play around with the Ferengi teeth, one of my favorite pastimes on *THE NEXT GENERATION*. After you've made one set of piranha teeth for a character, there's not much excitement in doing them over and over again. Instead, I decided to make each set of Ferengi teeth different from the others.

To create a new set of Ferengi teeth, I take a cast of the actor's mouth, the same way as I do with my Klingon actors. Once I have a plaster cast of the teeth, I start by placing individual, pointed acrylic teeth on the cast, leaving gaps between them, moving them closer together in some places, or even making double rows. I then take the cast of the lower teeth and align the upper and lower

"The Perfect Mate" Photo by Robbie Robinson: ©1992 Paramount Pictures

The Ferengi in "The Perfect Mate" had a lot of fun testing their custom teeth.

sets into each other. If I've left a gap in the upper row, I will fill it with a tooth coming up from the lower one, so when the actor talks, the teeth will open and close like his real teeth.

One of the amusing consequences of having a mouthful of misshapen teeth is that each of our Ferengi have a slight speech impediment. No matter how much you practice, there are certain things you just can't say properly. The teeth create more saliva in the actor's mouth, and give him that peculiar way of speaking.

Instead of trying to overcome the Ferengi's speech impediment, we actually decided to make it part of their characters. When we bring in a new actor, I try and explain that they're joining a long line of previous Ferengi, and I give them the new set of teeth several days ahead of time, so that like our Klingons, they can practice with them at home. There are letters that you can learn to say properly if you practice with them enough.

Some of our actors have a lot of fun with their new teeth, rehearsing in front of the mirror, and seeing what kind of expressions they can create for their characters. I remember one of our actors in "The Perfect Mate" who took his role very seriously. He had one tooth that stuck way out and actually made his lip curl a little bit. He had a great time,

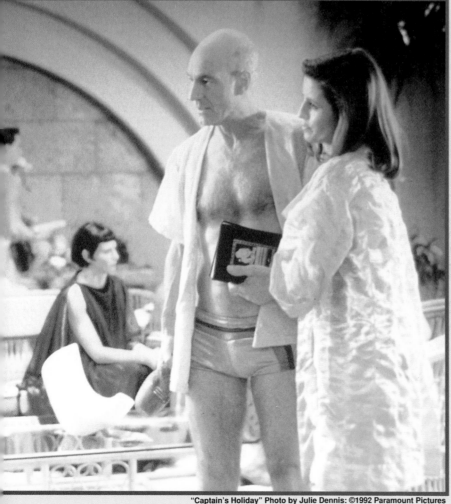

"Captain's Holiday" Photo by Julie Dennis: ©1992 Paramount Pictures

Picard and Vash (Jenifer Hetrick) are accosted by an annoying Ferengi (Max Grodenchik) in "Captain's Holiday."

Even though the same basic design is used for each Ferengi, Westmore allows each actor's own facial characteristics to create a unique individual.

putting the teeth in and practicing in front of the mirror. I thought he did a wonderful job.

Even though we use the same basic design for each of our Ferengi, I've found that the actor's own facial features lend their characters their individuality. A person's own eyes, his lips and the chin, which is not covered by an appliance, each give the Ferengi a slightly different look. Add the voice and the general

Designer Andy Probert created this original sketch of the Ferengi menace during the first season of ST:TNG.

shape of the face, and the characters become even more unique.

One thing that many people don't notice is that we use blue polish on the Ferengi's fingernails. It's difficult to see in many of their appearances, but if you can find a close-up of their hands, you'll notice that the fingernails have been painted a light, translucent blue color. We do that with all our Ferengi actors, except where the script calls for them to wear gloves.

If I had to pick a few of my favorite Ferengi, I think Frank Corsentino, who played DaiMon Tog in "Menage A Troi," did an excellent job. I remember thinking he would be a great Ferengi to bring back. I also liked Max Grodenchik, who appeared in "Captain's Holiday." He played Sovak, the Ferengi who spent most of the episode pestering Vash and Captain Picard. Max was great, and he did eventually return to the show. They've all been wonderful.

One of the best Ferengi we've done so far was in "Unification," where we had to make William Bastiani into a fat Ferengi trader. Instead of the usual facial appliances, we created a large piece that wrapped around his entire face. We made William up with a normal Ferengi head, and then took a facial cast of him. The new cheeks, jowls and nose were sculpted up so that they would blend in with the head piece, making him look fatter and more pig-like.

William was also the first Ferengi not to wear a symbol on his forehead; perhaps he never served on a Ferengi military ship.

Each time we bring back the Ferengi, I try to come up with something new for them, so they'll continue to remain fresh and interesting. In *Deep Space Nine*, I know the Ferengi characters, and I'm going to try and do something different with them; maybe design a face where the cheeks and nose are one single piece, or maybe put a scar here and there. Whatever we decide to do with them, the Ferengi are still a lot of fun to have around. ●

One of the questions most frequently asked by fans of *THE NEXT GENERATION* is, "When are the Borg coming back?" Although they've only been featured in four episodes during our first five seasons, the Borg have become one of our most popular alien life forms. There's something fundamentally unsettling about a race of emotionless creatures, who live only to assimilate other cultures, that seems to have struck a chord among our viewers.

When we first received the script for "Q-Who," the Borg's first appearance, it was obvious that the makeup and costume departments would have to work very closely in designing an effective look. Dorinda Wood, who was our costume designer on the second season, came up with a rough sketch that showed a man in a suit with tubes running around and attached to it. The head area she kept deliberately vague. The idea was that she would be responsible for the costume, and I would be responsible for the head, neck and exposed body areas.

Once the costume department selected the materials they wanted to use—a blackish, spandex-like fabric and a metallic urethane—I had to figure out a way to integrate the helmet with the rest of the body suit. I built the original helmets in the wardrobe department while they were working on the suits, so we could communicate with each other and make sure that our respective designs were meshing properly.

I made the heads out of foam rubber that would be comfortable

When Westmore received the script for "Q-Who," he knew that the costume and makeup departments would have to work closely in creating the Borg.

One of my favorite pastimes on ST:TNG is creating different eyepieces for the Borg.

helped make each head even more distinctive.

If we had a large exposed area of skin on the face or arm, I ran a tube directly into it. I created a latex appliance that looks like a little bullet hole which glues onto the skin, and the tube is glued right into the hole in the appliance. We had an actress in one episode who had a bare arm, and I ran several tubes into it to make her character look even more machine-like.

The actual makeup that we use on the Borg is a white base that blocks out all of the actor's natural skin tones. We wanted the Borg to look almost zombie-like, so the viewers would know they were seeing a creature that couldn't be reasoned or negotiated with, that they had been programmed for a single function from which it couldn't deviate. The white makeup was supposed to make the Borg look almost bloodless, as though the life had been leached out of them.

Once the makeup base has been applied, I take my airbrush and begin shadowing the face. I place shadows around the eyes to make them look even more life-

A few finishing touches are required for a Borg extra in "Q-Who."

for the actors to wear, and colored it to match the costume. Little clamps were added to the head piece, so we could take the tubing that was already sewn into the suits and run it directly around and into the helmets.

Next, I started covering the head appliances with little pieces of machinery. Originally, I used urethane parts that were cast from model kits, but eventually started experimenting with other materials that were more interesting to work with, such as old parts torn out of damaged electronic equipment. These extra pieces

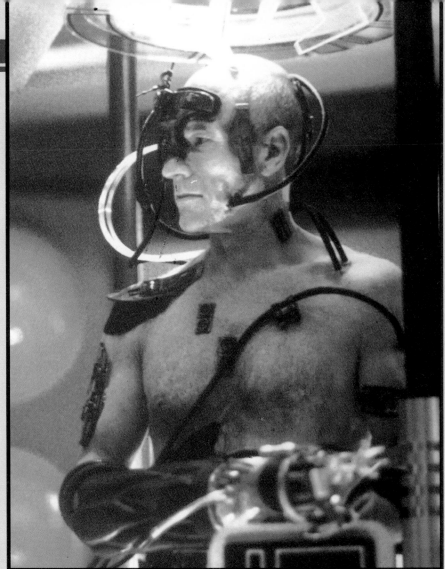

In "Best of Both Worlds," it took about two-and-a-half hours to transform Patrick Stewart into a Borg.

less, around the sides of the head where the helmet meets the face, and under the cheekbones and the back of the hands. I find that I can work much aster with an airbrush than by telling my makeup artist what to do. Where it would normally take someone 10 or 15 minutes to do the shadowing and blending by hand, I can do the same job with an airbrush in about two minutes. It also gives me 100 percent control over the actor's appearance. With two or more makeup artists working on their own, with their own techniques, it's very difficult to give each actor the same look.

Another thing that we established early on but didn't really show, was that the Borg were hairless. In that first episode, the helmets really didn't have too many openings and it was difficult to see the heads underneath, but that's something we changed in later appearances. I have several Borg heads now that have holes in them where you can see the bald skull beneath the helmet. If it's a particularly large area of exposed skin, I'll run a tube into it, so it looks like it's plugged right into the head.

One of my favorite pastimes on *THE NEXT GENERATION*, aside from making Ferengi teeth, is creating the different eyepieces for the Borg. Over the last several years, I've found countless sources of inspiration for new eyepieces—I've taken castings from binoculars, I've used pieces from model kits, I've added small crystal cubes to them; I've even found film cans in the trash,which I was able to put to good use.

One of the eyepieces I made for "The Best of Both Worlds" was made out of a flower stand left over from a testimonial dinner for Gene Roddenberry. The flowers at each table were stuck in an unusually-shaped centerpiece, and after the dinner was over, we took it home. A few days later, after the flowers had died, I was on my

way to work, and I found this centerpiece sitting in the trash. It was sticking up in the air, and I thought to myself, "I can use this!" I brought it to work with me, mounted a laser gun in the center of it, and put in on a female Borg. So much for the glamor of working in television!

Although the eyepieces look very elaborate and heavy, most of them are actually constructed from foam latex or a lightweight plastic. After they're painted black, I'll burnish everything with a metal paste.

The typical Borg makeup takes a little less than an hour to apply. The most time-consuming part is helping the actors get dressed. There are a lot of individual parts that the wardrobe department has to put on, a lot of tubing and so forth. If there's an exposed area of skin, such as an arm or a hand, we put the appliances on the actors before they get dressed.

Since each Borg was supposed to be part of a collective con-

sciousness, we decided to make the males and females look almost identical in appearance. The makeup and costumes are virtually the same, and sometimes you'd have to look very closely to determine the sex of the character. There are subtle clues that might give it away, such as the shape of a person's body underneath the uniform, or a slight softness in a woman's face, but basically, the look is the same.

We also had a scene in "Q-Who" that took place in a nursery, so we could show how the Borg start out as normal human infants and are gradually transformed by electronic implants. There's a wonderful shot of the Away Team standing in the nursery, and Riker pulls out a drawer in the wall, revealing an infant Borg. The baby belonged to Terry, our executive producer's secretary, who first had to bring the child in so I could take measurements of his head. Obviously, I wouldn't make a plaster cast of him, so I

"The Borg had been designed previously to my doing 'The Best of Both Worlds,' so the look was established," says director Cliff Bole. "I wanted to get some mechanics on his face, and the laser was Michael's idea. At the end of the show when Patrick was a Borg and that laser came off his head and flashed into camera, I thought that was very poignant and graphic."

used a doll's head of similar size to create the mold. I then made a tiny Borg headpiece that fitted the baby's real head, and my son created a small electronic gadget with blinking lights that adhered to his chest and helmet via two-way tape.

When we shot the nursery scene, we were only able to use the baby for a very short period of time, and had to have a nurse standing by because of his age. They had to do several takes, because each time the cameras started rolling, the baby would see the black cord that ran from his head to his chest, grab it, and start teething on it. Everyone thought it would be a wonderful idea to show the baby chewing on his cord, but they finally got one shot where he left the cord alone, and that was the one they used. I thought it was an effective scene, because it showed how the Borg started developing at a very early age.

When the Borg came back in the two-part story, "The Best of Both Worlds," we knew that there were going to be at least 10 or 12 actors to make up, and we had to find new ways of streamlining the process. One way was to create a basic headpiece that could be altered to fit more than one actor. I designed a helmet that had one opening in the back of the neck, one in the top of the head, one in the front where the forehead is and one on each side. I then made a series of little covers that fit over each opening. I could either close up the entire head, or by removing different covers, expose as much of the head as I wanted. This gave me the flexibility of making different heads from one mold.

I also created a large quantity of new facial appliances which could be used in different combinations. I made black implants for the chin and cheeks, the nose and upper lips. These large appliances

are colored to blend in with the headpiece, and tubing could be attached to them.

Before we started filming, each headpiece was pre-painted, as were all the little bits and implants that had to be glued to the face. I made up a number of special eyepieces, so we were able to mix and match a different combination for each actor.

One of our biggest challenges in "The Best of Both Worlds" was transforming Patrick Stewart into a Borg. When Picard is captured and brought aboard the alien ship, there was a scene where they started operating on him, and we had to show his humanity gradually being drained away. We started by making him a little paler, though he never actually got to a full white Borg makeup. It took about two-and-a-half hours to lighten up his entire body for that scene.

The next time we see Picard is when the Away Team transports over to the Borg ship to rescue

The Borg Locutus

The Borg character style was familiar to me, because we had met them before, The problem with the makeup was that I had to be identifiably Borg and also identifiably Jean-Luc Picard; I had to balance that in such a way that the audience never lost the sense that somewhere behind this semi-mechanical creature, there was the human being that the

audience had known for three or four years. The skin color was significant, because the deathlike appearance, the almost metallic looking skin did more to help me feel the lack of the humanity of the character.

The other thing that Michael came up with was the laser beam attached to the side of my head. It hadn't been used with any of the other Borg, and it added to the hi-tech dimension of the character. I think that was what made the character of Locutus so intimidating, in terms of appearance.

I always use the makeup time in the theatre as a way of immersing myself in the character. By the time the makeup is done and the costume goes on, I don't have to work at finding who I am. The process was the same with all three major makeups that Michael has done for me, watching it go on, and feeling the changes happen on a visceral level. Once it was on, particularly with the Borg makeup and costume which were very restrictive. I couldn't stand, I couldn't move, I couldn't speak the same way, so it was a sense of emotional deadness that developed with the application of the makeup.
—Patrick Stewart

him, only to find that he has already been transformed into one of the robotic creatures. For Patrick's full Borg makeup, we gave him a partial headpiece that wrapped around the back and covered his right eye. There was a tube that ran into his brain, and several tubes were connected to his body.

On the front of Patrick's headpiece, my son built a little sweeping mechanism that went over the right eye. It was connected to a servo motor, and the batteries to run it were mounted to the back of his head. The wires ran from back to front, but were virtually invisible, because they were entwined with the rest of the gadgetry on the headpiece. We had a remote control unit off-camera, one of those devices used for model airplanes, and were able to make the little sweeper rotate back and forth.

The other major innovation with Patrick was mounting a small laser beam on the side of his headpiece, next to his right eye, something which really hadn't been done before. *Predator* used

Riker and Crusher investigate the Borg's crash site in "I-Borg."

them before us, but we were the first television program to experiment with lasers.

The idea for using a laser was the result of a conversation I had with my son about what we could do to make Patrick's Borg character visually exciting. Originally, we thought of putting some blinking

lights on the headpiece, but Michael, Jr., said, "Let me see if I can find a mini-laser, and what we can do with it." He researched the idea, made a few calls, and came up with a small laser that was only one inch long. He then built the holding chamber for it, and a little on-off switch, and we incorporated the entire unit into the headpiece.

Since we were dealing with a device that hadn't been filmed for television before, we weren't quite sure how it would photograph. One problem was that if there was no smoke on the set, it would be difficult to see the sweep of the laser beam, but Marvin Rush, our director of photography, was a big help. He blew smoke into the chamber, and it worked beautifully.

The other effect we wanted to try was at the end of "Best of Both Worlds—Part I," when Patrick looks directly into the camera, and the laser beam points toward the viewer. We had no idea how it would look, but we told the camera man not to stare into the lens once the shot was set up. We

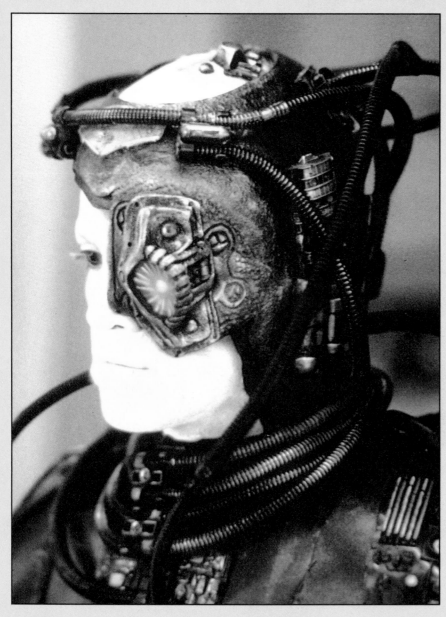

ing needed to make the effect work.

The second challenge that had to be solved was a scene where Geordi asks Jonathan's character, who he christens "Hugh," if he could take a look at the Borg's eyepiece. Hugh reaches up, pulls off the piece and hands it to him. The question I had to ask myself was what do you see when a Borg pulls his eye out? When I started designing the eyepiece, I built magnets into both sides of the appliance, so it would click together. The magnets had holes in the center, and my son built a four-colored LED, so when Hugh pulls off his eyepiece, a series of red, green, yellow and orange lights started blinking. We hooked the LEDs to a battery pack on the actor's back, and ran the wires inside the head piece.

We also created an arm for Jonathan that was a little different from the arms that had previously been created by the property department. The other Borg arms were very heavy, with whirring motors on the end, but since we were dealing with a young creature of about 18 years old, I didn't want to weigh him down with a heavy, clublike limb. What I did was design an arm made out of foam rubber which reached up to the elbow and slipped on and off like a glove. Michael, Jr.'s electronics were hooked up with a male/female attachment that I could unplug and let him out of when he needed to take a break.

Instead of a thumb, I built a sharp, rotating extension shaped a bit like a rocketship, which looked extremely lethal. On the outside of the hand, where the little finger is, I added an attachment with which Hugh could literally plug himself into the Enterprise's electrical system. If you look closely, you can see it in the scene where he plugs himself into the wall to replenish his energy levels.

Jonathan's makeup only took about 45 minutes to apply, but it took a lot of time to get him into

filmed the scene without doing any tests, and then had to wait until the dailies came out the next day to see the results. To our delight, the laser effect worked just as we had hoped, giving us a memorable shot to end the third season.

The Borg didn't return until the end of the fifth season, in "I, Borg." We knew this story was going to present some interesting challenges, because it focused on a young Borg (played by Jonathan Del Arco) who was brought back to the Enterprise by the Away Team. It was the first time we had an episode with a Borg as a principal character, and we knew there were going to be a

lot of close-ups on him.

We tried a lot of new ideas with Jonathan's Borg character—I mentioned earlier how much I enjoyed creating the Borg eyepieces, and for this episode I wanted to come up with something special. I had been out shopping with my wife Marion around Christmastime, and we came across a holographic store which had some very interesting items. I remember thinking to myself, "Gee, it might be nice to use one of these on a character someday," and when we started working on this story, I recalled some of the holograms would change as they were seen from different angles. Again, Marvin Rush was a big help, providing the proper overhead light-

the costume, slip the glove on and plug in the motors for his hand. It was a lot of work, but well worth it when we saw how it looked on screen. There were some wonderful close-ups of Jonathan in that episode, and we were all thrilled with the way it turned out.

There were a few dead Borg characters in "I, Borg" seen in the beginning of the episode, and in the final scene. There's a very good shot at the end, where we see a dead Borg lying on the ground, and a panel was blown off his helmet, exposing the brain underneath. The appliance was actually created for an experimental play I worked on last year in California called *Hence Forward.* The main character has created a robot to take the place of his wife, and at the end of the first act, he whips off the robot's wig, revealing her bald head. He pushes her forward, and opens up her head to make some adjustments. As he turns on a little switch, the house lights go down. All you see on the stage is this little pattern of blinking lights, and you finally realize that you're seeing into the robot's head.

I took the head design which had been used in this play, and worked it into the Borg story. It was an interesting effect I'd like to try using again the next time we go back to Borgville. It might be fun to show a live Borg with a clear cover over the top of his head, so you can see the brain with some feeder tubes running into it, and maybe we'll put some smoke in it, or even a little bladder to make it pulsate.

We've already got plenty of ideas in mind for the Borg's next appearance. I thought the laser we built for Patrick worked really well, and my son and I have already discussed a few ways of using lasers in the future. Because the Borg are so alien in nature, we can do almost anything with them that our imaginations can create, and I'm looking forward to their future appearances. Who knows what ideas we'll come up with? ●

The Cardassians

The Cardassians were given a scaly, lizard-like appearance to emphasize their alien nature.

Halfway through our fourth season on THE NEXT GENERATION, I was asked to create a new species of humanoids called the Cardassians. Like the Romulans, they were supposed to be a nasty, untrustworthy race of creatures, but like the Klingons, we wanted to make them distinctly different from humans, with their own identities and their own unique set of physical characteristics.

The first thing we decided to do was give the Cardassians a scaly, lizard-like appearance to emphasize their alien nature. We also colored their skin a cold grey which fell short of looking metallic, but gave the impression of being rough and armored. As I started sculpting the heads, I continued to emphasize those reptilian qualities, adding ridges and bumps to the skin and making subtle alterations to the face, ears and head. I created a twin row of bony ridges which started from the peak of the eyebrows and ran all the way back into the hairline. Ridges went down the sides of the neck and flared out to the shoulder tips, giving the Cardassians a strange, menacing appearance, like a preying mantis or a king cobra. The idea was to hire people with long, thin necks that accentuated that look, starting with their first appearance in "The Wounded."

The final Cardassian makeup requires an impressive number of appliances for the face and head. There's a forehead piece, two pieces for the sides of the neck, and two more pieces that hook onto the earlobes and come across the jawline. We also added a small appliance under the tip of the nose, and another for the front of the chin and neck area.

Because the Cardassians are a semi-reptilian race, we tried to de-emphasize their hair; instead of giving them wigs, we merely slicked the hair back tight against the head. Only one of the characters so far has had a moustache—that was Mark Alaimo in the first story. I didn't want them to look too hairy, but sometimes an actor needs a little something extra on their face.

In terms of applying the makeup, it takes two people, working on the same actor, about two-and-a-half hours. They start on the forehead, anchoring it down in the middle, and each person begins working simultaneously on a different side of the head. If one person had to turn out a Cardassian by himself, it would probably take four hours on the first day, and maybe three hours after that, once he knew where to put everything without having to stop and think.

As we were creating the look of the Cardassians, I tried to work closely with costume designer Bob Blackman, so that his ideas would support what I was trying to do with the makeup. Because the characters had a wide, flared neck, Bob had to make sure that the costumes were designed to accommodate that look. He also picked up on our theme of making the Cardassians strong and menacing by creating a series of armored costumes for them, which worked beautifully.

creating brand new head pieces for each character, I want to find subtler ways of changing the existing pieces, perhaps widening the forehead ridges or making them larger. The basic structure would stay the same, but we would create variations on the same theme.

I'm very excited about doing more with the Cardassians on *DEEP SPACE NINE,* because I think it's one of the most effective

When the Cardassians returned in "Ensign Ro," we used the same basic design that had been created for their first appearance. Again, it was important to find actors with the proper physical characteristics to make the characters work: A long neck and a sharp, angular face that lent itself to the makeup. As with the Ferengi, who also have a large part of their face covered with appliances, we depend on the unique features of the Cardassian actors to make each of them different.

Although we've only used the Cardassians twice in *THE NEXT GENERATION,* they will be playing a big part in our spinoff series, *DEEP SPACE NINE.* Since they'll probably be getting a lot of screen time, I want to redesign their makeup, giving the facial appliances more depth and detail,

so they'll be more visually exciting. The basic design is still good, but I feel that like our other recurring aliens, we have to keep finding new ways of improving them and making them interesting. It's not a matter of making drastic changes, just enhancing the design we've already created.

Because the Cardassians' makeup is already so complicated, I don't want to fall into the same trap on the new series that I did with the Klingons five years ago of having to make each head piece totally different. Instead of

and exciting alien makeups we've ever created for *THE NEXT GENERATION.* There are still so many things to try—for instance, we haven't seen a Cardassian's hands yet; up until now, they've always worn gloves. If we ever get to see their hands, it might be fun to make them more bony, a little bit of segmentation that ties in with the bony shape of the face and neck. Whatever we decide to do, I have a feeling the Cardassians will soon become a major force in the *STAR TREK* universe, and one of our most popular alien races. ●

Some of the Klingon foreheads in *ST:TNG* are created by using sections of dinosaur vertebrae as a reference.

When we first started talking about using the Klingons in *THE NEXT GENERATION,* I wanted to do something different from the previous series, as well as the *STAR TREK* films. Until now, Klingons were brown. Some had a bony ridge running down the middle of their foreheads, long black wigs and facial hair, and I felt that for such a fierce warrior race, copying old designs just wasn't enough for *THE NEXT GENERATION.* I wanted to lend a little more ferocity to their overall appearance, so I asked Rick Berman and Gene Roddenberry to let me try something different from what "had gone before."

As I started designing the makeup for Michael Dorn (Worf), our main Klingon character, one of my biggest changes was adding a latex nose which flowed down from his forehead, bringing the ridged look into the middle of his face. The nose appliance covers the bridge of the nose, adding a sharp ridge to it, and connects into the forehead piece. The idea turned out to be quite successful and became one of our signatures on the series, one of the clear differences between what we were doing with the Klingons and what had been done in the past.

Each one of our Klingon actors has a latex nose made for him, so in addition to the huge backlog of different foreheads we've accumulated over the years, there is a supply of different noses as well. Even Worf's son Alexander has a tiny little latex nose that fits over his own.

After incorporating a nose piece into the design, I created a set of Klingon teeth for Michael, making them look broken and discolored, something else the films haven't done. The teeth are acrylic caps that fit over the actor's own teeth, giving them that uneven look. Each set is custom-made for the actor; this allows them to fit perfectly, and like real teeth, no set looks exactly alike. I give them to the actors a day or two before they start working, so they can practice speaking with them.

As I started sculpting the first forehead pieces for our Klingon guest stars, I was under the mis-

"The Icarus Factor" Photo: ©1989 Paramount Pictures

Brian Thompson as Lt. Klag and Christopher Collins as Captain Kargan played Klingons in "A Matter of Honor."

"A Matter of Honor" Photo: ©1989 Paramount Pictures

John Tesh of *Entertainment Tonight* guest-starred as a Klingon in "The Icarus Factor."

taken impression that each design had to be different, as opposed to using the same mold more than once. It was the beginning of what I would eventually call "Klingon Hell"; the self-imposed task of sculpting a new and different head for virtually every Klingon actor who works on *THE NEXT GENERATION*. By the end of the fifth season, I have probably sculpted more than 30 individual heads.

The process of casting the actor's head, making a mold from it, and sculpting the elaborate bone structure, generally takes about two days. In the case of a story like "Redemption," which had a large cast of Klingon characters, we had to develop a series of shortcuts to save time. Instead of

Riker discovers the problems of serving on a Klingon ship in "A Matter of Honor."

making a cast of each actor's head for example, I would measure their head when they walked in the door. If their head size was close to that of a pre-existing mold, we would create our new design on an available head mold.

Quite often, if we had two actors with similarly-sized heads, I would sculpt the first forehead design, and after taking a mold from it, the clay sculpture would still be intact. This would eliminate the need for "basing it up"; the process of putting the clay on the mold. By saving that time, I'm able to start redesigning a new bone structure for the second Klingon right away. Instead of spending an entire day on the new sculpture, I can re-sculpt the second in three or four hours.

Each Klingon character has to be made-up for natural lighting conditions, no matter what the script calls for.

of his with the same facial features, the mold goes into storage, never to be seen again.

Once the actors are made up, with the forehead and nose, wigs are applied. With the background Klingons, we use inexpensive wigs—by inexpensive, I mean from $60 up to $300 each—which are usually hot glued onto the headpieces. If the actor is playing a background character and is only involved in a few days' filming, the wig is glued to the headpiece on day one after the makeup is applied. That night, when we take off his makeup, the head is carefully removed with the wig and makeup still attached, and the fine edges of the forehead appliance are cleaned up so it can be reused the following day. It saves time the next morning for the hairdressers who don't have to reattach the wigs, and for makeup artists who would normally have to make-up a new head.

With principal Klingons such as Worf, we use a more expensive hair lace wig, which is individually glued on by the hairstylist before the actor goes on camera. At the end of the day, the wig is removed, and the hairdresser "blocks it," meaning that it's pinned onto a head block, curlers are rolled into it, and redressed

Believe it or not, the way I create the elaborate forehead designs is by looking at sections of dinosaur vertebrae. There are several books that I used as reference material; one book in particular on the anatomy of dinosaurs is absolutely marvelous. I can come up with any number of different ideas just by isolating a small portion of a single vertebrae. Many of those ideas eventually find their way onto the top of a Klingon head.

Although each of our principal Klingons has a different forehead design, I can sometimes recycle those heads for use in crowd scenes where a large number of background Klingons are needed. In some cases though, a design is just too elaborate to use again. With a character like K'mpec, for example, or Ambassador Kell from "The Mind's Eye," the heads are so distinct that they have to be "retired" from use, because they are too recognizable. Unless the character returns in a future episode, or maybe a close relative

Michael Dorn on Worf

"We've done over 600 makeups so far; that's a lot of makeups," Michael Dorn says. "There is a lot of Worf in me, but when you have a mask, you can do just about anything you want to. It's a difficult makeup, but it does keep you in the Worf mode.

"The actual makeup takes about an hour and a half. I usually occupy myself in the morning by reading the paper. Gerry Quist has done my makeup so many times by now, I can usually sit there with my paper open, and he's able to work around it.

"The hardest part about Worf's makeup is the glue. I had major problems with it in the second year, and I really thought I was going to have to quit. I didn't want to, but my face couldn't take it. I went to the producers and said, 'Look, I love the show, I love my character and I love doing it, but my skin is going crazy!' They sat down and changed a lot of things, and made it a lot easier for me to work.

"I liked the way they lengthened the hair over the last few years, but with most of the hairdressers we've been using, they see long hair and they start to curl it, so it looks like Prince Valiant, which doesn't fit. This year, I hope we're going to get a hairstyle that we all like—something that's easy and also fits the character. I wanted a long, long pony tail that would come down and around, where you could put some ornaments on it. It would be easy, and it would also keep the hair out of the face."

—*Michael Dorn*

A gauntlet of Holodeck-created Klingons awaits Worf in "The Icarus Factor."

K'Ehleyr's half-human and half-Klingon makeup reflects her heritage.

Renegade Klingons stir things up on the *Enterprise* in "Heart of Glory."

K'Ehleyr tries out Worf's exercise program in "The Emissary."

for the next day. The cost for a fine hair lace wig is about $2,500.

Michael's hair originally started out with a short wig, which was Gene Roddenberry's idea. He wanted Worf to have a military hairstyle like everyone else, but a strange thing happened. When Richard Sabre, our original hairstylist, left the series, his successor let Michael Dorn's hair drop a little longer, and the next, longer still. The production office would say, "Oh, that looks OK," and the hair would continue to grow. The fans loved it, because they could almost tell when the series was filmed just by looking at the length of Worf's hair. They could watch an episode and say, "Ah, this is from season three."

After the hairstylists have glued the wigs on, the actors return to the makeup department so the makeup artists can add the beards and moustaches. That's another thing I try to do with the Klingons: Making each of them look different in terms of their facial hair goods. There are so many things that can be done with the facial hair that we're constantly able to come up with new and interesting combinations. One of my favorites is Gowron, the leader of the Klingon empire. We had a lot of fun with his makeup, giving him a beard that comes down the sides of his face and across the moustache. There's another one I remember where I designed the moustache like a set of crab pincers, so when he opened his mouth they would separate, and when he closed it, they came together. I created that one by twisting the moustache under the jawline, and then taking hair styling gel and bringing the points together. The facial hair is just as important to the design of the Klingons as the foreheads.

Although we try to make each of our Klingon characters different, there have been a few occasions when members of the same family have appeared together. In those instances, I try to create variations on a single theme, using the same basic head design, but subtly altering it for each character. The best example that comes to mind is the Duras family. When we introduced Lursa and B'Etor, the two sisters in "Redemption," I tried to use the same crab-shaped design for their foreheads as I had originally created for their brother Duras, as played by Patrick Massett. I used the same concept with Toral (J.D. Cullum), who was Duras' son, and had to bear some resemblance to his deceased father.

We tried a similar approach with Worf's Klingon family, using Michael Dorn's design as the starting point. It began with Tony Todd, who played Worf's brother Kurn in the third season story, "Sins of the Father." Tony's fore-

Alexander's Klingon headpiece is a miniature version of Worf's.

Jonathan Frakes directs Klingon Jon Steuer (as Alexander) in "Reunion."

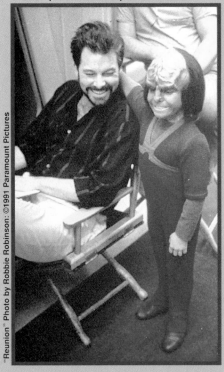

parents: Worf, his father, and K'ehleyr, his mother. The problem was that K'Ehleyr, played by Suzie Plakson, was supposed to be half-human/half-Klingon, and her makeup had to reflect that combination. The bone structure on her forehead was very subtle, and the production team wanted to keep her attractive, so I didn't put a nosepiece on her, or give her a set of Klingon teeth. We then gave her a light tan skin tone, so that her features were more visible and human-looking.

Anyway, when I first designed K'Ehleyr's head, I had no idea that she would have a child one season later, and the bone structure was so subtle that I wasn't able to incorporate it into Alexander's head. The answer, I finally realized, was to make him look like a miniature version of Worf. He has the same type of headpiece as Michael, and as I mentioned earlier, a small nose appliance.

To reflect his mother's influence, I used a shade of brown for his skin color called ST-1, which is lighter than Michael's, but darker than Suzie's. We also decided not to give him a set of Klingon teeth. He looked more like his mother without them, and they would have been difficult for a small boy. With a huge mouthful of teeth, Alexander would have wound up looking like a Ferengi.

While the part of Worf's son was originally played by Jon Steuer in "Reunion," he was eventually replaced by Brian Bonsall, who many people remember from his days on *Family Ties*. Rather than changing Brian's makeup when he joined the show, we applied the head and nose pieces on him that were designed for Jon. While we were able to use the same sized appliances throughout the fifth season, Brian eventually started to outgrow them, and we had to make a new head for Alexander at the start of season six.

Some viewers have wondered how we handle the makeup for fair-skinned actors playing Klingons, as opposed to black actors. The way

the production team settled that from the very beginning was that Michael Dorn and actors with natural brown skin tones would be considered Northern Klingons, and fair-skinned actors would be Southern Klingons.

With a black actor, instead of trying to lighten his skin tone, we match his own natural color to the headpiece. On a fair-skinned person, we use a shade called desert tan. It gives us a smooth continuity in skin color, and allows us to do a lot of shading and stippling. So far, the fairest Klingon we've had on *THE NEXT GENERATION* was Suzie Plakson's K'Ehleyr, who was supposed to be half-human.

Whenever we make up a Klingon character, we have to assume that he will be filmed under natural lighting conditions, whether the script says he will be standing on the brightly-lit Bridge of the *Enterprise*, or under the dim red lights of a Klingon ship. We may be shooting on several different sets on a given day, and since there's no time for makeup changes in-between, our actors have to be ready for anything.

On the other hand, there are so many shadows on those Klingon ships, and so much subdued lighting, that a lot of our subtle effects won't show up. If there's a scene where a Klingon is getting killed, for instance, we have to make the wounds large enough so that the viewer knows the character has been killed.

I remember we had to do a scene on one of the Klingon ships,

head piece was similar to Michael's, but had to be cut down in size, because Michael's actual head is much bigger. In addition, Tony's nose is longer, which meant that his character's face would look different.

The character of Alexander took a little more thought. He had to have the features of both his

Political intrigue in the Klingon council chamber was the focus for "Redemption."

Fek'lhr (Thad Lamey) was the Klingon demon created for "Devil's Due."

Westmore tries to make each Klingon look different by coming up with new combinations of facial hair.

Gowron was one of Westmore's most elaborate Klingon makeups in "Redemption."

and the shot had to start with a Klingon slumped over a console with a piece of shrapnel stuck in his head. I used a piece of mirrored plastic with a lot of futuristic computer-type things glued to it, and I was putting the different Klingons in their makeup chairs and giving instructions. I took the one Klingon into the trailer and said to the makeup artist, "This one's going to be dead. Here's the piece of machinery I want embedded in his face; we'll cut the appliances here, and then apply the blood." I then went about my business, making the rounds of the three places where our Klingons were being made up, and making sure that everything was progressing.

I walked into the lab where some of the background Klingons were being made up (the individual who was supposed to be killed was a background Klingon, by the way) and it suddenly dawned on me that one of these men who looked perfectly healthy was supposed to be the dead one. I had gotten the two actors mixed up!

I ran back to the trailer just as they were getting ready to shoot, and the Klingon who was not supposed to be dead was walking down the steps, with this big chunk of shrapnel embedded in his face, and blood running down. I looked at him and said, "You're not supposed to be dead!" He said, "I didn't think so," and had apparently been telling the makeup artist all along, "I don't think I'm supposed to be dead!" Very quickly, I pulled this piece of plastic out of his head, rushed him into the trailer, and told the artist girl to take the blood off. We cleaned him up, and where the shrapnel had been embedded in his head, we turned the hole into a large scar which looked great. I then ran back to the other room where the "dead" guy was waiting, and I put two of my people to work, embedding the piece of broken console in his face and bloodying him up for the shot. We brought him onto the set, and they did the scene.

On some of the big Klingon shows like "Sins of The Father" or "Redemption," things can get pretty hectic, with so much work to be done in a relatively short period of time. In order to maintain the show's unusually high level of quality, it's very important to hire enough extra hands to meet the demands of the story.

In the case of "Redemption," we had more than 25 Klingons to make-up, which meant hiring an extra 12 people for that week. We started working on the first group of Klingons at four in the morning, and had 12 of them ready to shoot

The Duras family joins up with the Romulans in "Redemption II."

We started at four in the morning, and for the next 12 hours, my makeup crew and I stayed in the trailer as the people lined up outside. We glued blisters, made burns, applied scars, dirtied them down; they had to bring our food to us, because we never left that trailer. The shot started with Steve Guttenberg and Lori Lethin in the center of the gymnasium, and they kept making the shot wider as we got more people ready. By the end of the day, the last extra was finished, and they were able to film the master shot with all 1,500 people.

With the amount of time it takes to turn a person into a Klingon, it's easy to think that most actors would find the two-and-a-half hour process uncomfortable, to say the least. Strangely enough, I've found the opposite to be true. Most of our guest stars, Klingon or otherwise, come in expecting a good time, and for seven or eight days, they get to play something they wouldn't normally get to do. There are a few actors who might sit and grumble a bit, but I would say they number less than one percent. The rest do it because they get to be seen on *STAR TREK.*

As far as our Klingon guest stars, I remember when John Tesh, one of the hosts of *Entertainment Tonight*, came in to do an episode. He was in the final

by 6:30am. We then started on our second group, and had them all finished by 9:30am.

The difference between working on *THE NEXT GENERATION* and a full-length feature film is that on a film, they would hire 25 makeup artists and get everyone made up at once. On a television show, you're able to design your shots around the number of people who are ready for shooting.

A good example of how a crowd scene is handled on another TV film is when I was working on *The Day After.* There was one shot where the camera pulls back to show 1,500 people covering the floor of a basketball gymnasium at the University of Kansas, and each one of them was wearing casualty makeup.

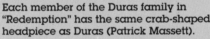

Each member of the Duras family in "Redemption" has the same crab-shaped headpiece as Duras (Patrick Massett).

Brian Bonsall took over the role of Alexander in "New Ground."

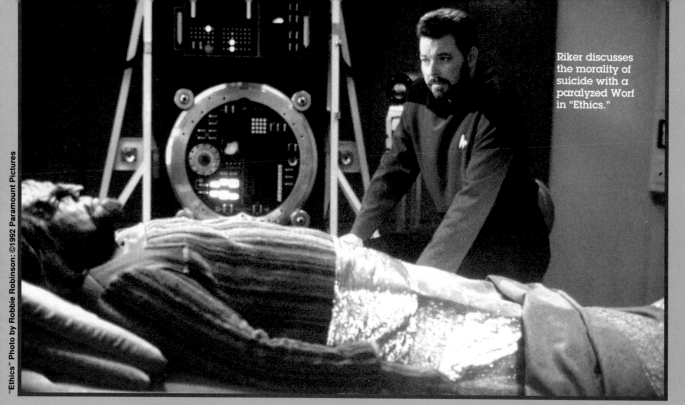

Riker discusses the morality of suicide with a paralyzed Worf in "Ethics."

A lesson in Klingon physiology was delivered in "Ethics."

scene of "The Icarus Factor," playing one of the Klingons on the Holodeck. John came over from his own show, I made him up, and after they shot Worf's torture scene, I had to clean him up so he could get back to *Entertainment Tonight.* There's something about our show that brings out the child or fan in everybody.

One of the reasons I still find the Klingons so interesting, even after five years, is because we're always doing something new and interesting with them. In "Ethics," for instance, one of the stories we did near the end of season five, we finally revealed what a Klingon's back looked like, something which had never been seen in *STAR TREK*'s 25-year history. For that scene, in which Worf's entire spinal column is removed, we also had to create a Klingon spine, which was based on the length of Michael's real spine. For every two human vertebrae, there was only a single Klingon vertebrae.

At the base of the removed spine, I had to build a small brain which controls the lower part of the Klingon's body. If you look closely during the surgery scene, you can see the auxiliary brain attached to the bottom of the spinal column.

We even showed what a Klingon's feet looked like towards the end of that episode. There's a scene where Worf is struggling to walk, and since the producers wanted him to be barefoot, they asked me to do something different with his feet. I devised a series of spines that ran down the front of his feet as well as an appliance that looked like a small horn. It's only a quick shot, but I thought it was very effective.

As for the future, there's still a lot about the Klingons that we haven't explored yet. They're an important part of the *STAR TREK* universe, and I'm looking forward to doing new and exciting things with them in the years to come. ●

Westmore created the Klingon vertebrae in "Ethics."

The Vulcans

The Mintakans are designed to be Vulcans at a primitive stage of their evolution.

Although the Vulcans have been an important part of the *STAR TREK* universe since the very beginning, their appearances in *THE NEXT GENERATION* have been somewhat limited. Because of their importance to the original series, we didn't want to invite comparison by putting a Vulcan on the bridge of the new *Enterprise* for example, or by introducing major Vulcan characters. The idea was for *THE NEXT GENERATION* to establish its own identity, and we couldn't do that by relying too heavily on the past.

However, the Vulcans *were* an important part of our universe, and we tried to acknowledge that by slipping them into a scene in Ten-Forward, or having a Vulcan walk down a corridor during a shot. It was important to remind our viewers that there were many different races on board the *Enterprise*, and I had a lot of fun making up the occasional extra as a Vulcan and putting him in the background. I remember one episode where my daughter McKenzie got to play a Vulcan extra—it was a real thrill for her to come on the show and get to wear pointed ears.

Our first major Vulcan character was the student who appeared in "Coming of Age," competing against Wesley Crusher in the Starfleet entrance exam. It wasn't a large part, but the viewers were reminded of the Vulcans' presence in our universe. A few months later, we followed that up with another Vulcan; Henry Darrow, who played a Vulcan admiral taken over by the alien parasites in the "Conspiracy."

No additional aging effects were added to Mark Lenard as Sarek, opting to go with the look from the feature films instead.

When Sarek returned in "Unification," his makeup was slightly changed to suggest the effects of his debilitating illness.

In the second season story, "The Schizoid Man," we introduced Dr. Selar, a Vulcan medical officer, played by Suzie Plakson. Suzie had the unusual distinction of being the only guest star in THE NEXT GENERATION to play both a Vulcan and a Klingon; a few months after appearing as Dr. Selar, she returned as K'Ehleyr, Worf's Klingon love interest in "The Emissary." For Suzie's Vulcan character, we used the standard LN-1 makeup base that I mentioned earlier for the Romulans. We try to keep the Vulcans a light yellow color, avoiding any red highlights that would photograph as natural skin tones. We also use the banged hairstyle that was introduced in the original STAR TREK series.

Many people have asked me if we custom-make a pair of ears for every actor who plays a Vulcan on the show, or if they come in one standard size. For the first few seasons, I did make new ears for each character, but we eventually built up a series of many different sizes, so that if an actor came in who had a medium-sized ear, I would have a medium Vulcan ear that fit, and so on. Every actor who plays a Vulcan has to be pre-fitted because every once in a while, a new size or shape has to be made.

Every pair of Vulcan eyebrows is also different. Some might be dark and heavy, while others might be lighter and sparser. The different combinations add further individuality to each Vulcan or Romulan character.

I tried to design the ears so that they would be unobtrusive and not draw attention away from the character. When we went to see STAR TREK VI, I actually found myself watching Leonard Nimoy's ears, because they were really interesting, and different from the ones we did on THE NEXT GENERATION. Our ears are modeled after a mid-version Leonard: Not too narrow, with a rounder point. We also use the same ears on all our Romulan characters.

Getting back to "The Schizoid Man," there were a few lines in the script where Dr. Graves mentions Selar's attractiveness, so in addition to her Vulcan features, we had to make her look attractive at the same time. I used a little eye makeup to bring out her eyes, and a brown-toned lipstick and blush that would lend itself to the yellowish Vulcan skin tone.

Once our series had been well established, we felt more comfortable bringing back some of the established Vulcan characters. First, Mark Lenard appeared in THE NEXT GENERATION as Sarek, bridging the gap between the STAR TREK films and the new series. Since Vulcans are

Leonard Nimoy as Spock was the role model for the Vulcans in *ST:TNG*.

Most people actually remember "Unification" for the appearance of Leonard Nimoy as Spock, the role model for all our Vulcan characters in *THE NEXT GENERATION*. Leonard came in straight from his work on *STAR TREK VI*, which had just finished filming, and he brought makeup artist Michael Mills with him. Michael had done Leonard's makeup for the film, and used the same Spock makeup for *THE NEXT GENERATION*.

Again, since there was only an 80-year gap between the last film and the time period of the series, it was decided that Spock should look basically the same. I'm sure it was a technical point that didn't make any difference to the millions of people who watched "Unification."

We also created a race of proto-Vulcans for the third-season story "Who Watches the Watchers?" They were called the Mintakans, and they were supposed to be like Vulcans at a more primitive stage in their evolution. They had the same pointed ears, but the eyebrows were heavier, and went up at a more outward angle than the normal Vulcan eyebrows. They had a forehead piece too, which wasn't as severe as a Romulan's forehead, but was supposed to give them a more prehistoric look.

Because the Federation was studying the development of the Mintakans, the script called for Troi and Riker to disguise themselves as two of the primitive villagers. We used the same makeup design for them as we did for the other Mintakans, and changed Marina Sirtis's curly wig, for a shorter, bobbed hairstyle. We also put a wig on Jonathan Frakes to cover his normal military hair cut.

Now that the Vulcans have become more prominent on *THE NEXT GENERATION*, I hope we'll be seeing more of them. I don't know if Spock will ever return, but it would be nice to see some scripts that featured a few Vulcans in prominent roles. They are old friends after all, and it's always nice to see old friends after they've been gone a long time. ●

supposed to live extremely long lives, they reasoned that Sarek would still be living long and prospering in our universe.

The first time Mark came in, we decided not to do any real aging on him, opting for the look of the films instead. The studio thought it would be better to simply use the natural lines and contours of Mark's face and leave it at that. I also made a new pair of ears for him that had character to match his regular features.

When Mark returned in "Unification," we did change his makeup slightly, to show the effects of the debilitating illness his character had been suffering. We used the same basic design as in "Sarek," but added some shadowing and rubber stretching around the eyes to suggest fatigue.

The two generations of *TREK*: Spock meets Picard, who is disguised as a Romulan.

Henry Darrow
appeared as one
of the early
Vulcans in the
first season story,
"Conspiracy."

The Holodeck

There were no restrictions placed on creating Worf's Holodeck opponents in "The Emissary."

One of the most fascinating aspects of the *Enterprise*'s Holodecks is their ability to recreate any imaginable environment, whether it's the jungle landscape of a distant planet, or some period of Earth's history. From a makeup artist's point-of-view, it's given me the chance to create an unbelievable collection of characters. Over the last several years, we've been able to populate the world of Dixon Hill ("The Big Goodbye"), return to the London of Sherlock Holmes ("Elementary, Mr Dear Data"), and fill a hall with a gauntlet of Klingons ("The Icarus Factor"). On the Holodeck, there are no rules, other than those of our imaginations.

The longest running characters I created for the Holodeck are the alien warriors in Worf's exercise program, first seen in "Where Silence Has Lease." There were no restrictions, so I wanted to do something a little more frightening, such as the skull-faced being or the insect creature.

My favorite Holodeck sequence was in "The Cost of Living," which recently received an Emmy Award for its makeup. I was able

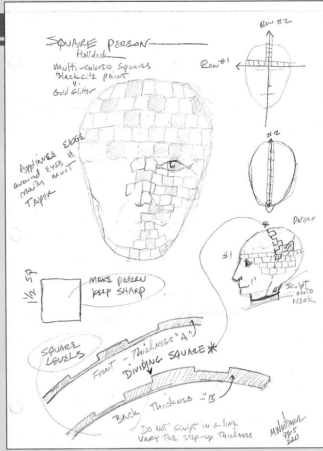

The mud baths in "Cost of Living" were populated by a group of strange, whimsical creatures.

The Wind Dancer head from "Cost of Living" was covered with little, colored squares and sculpted separations to create a three-dimensional texture.

had to be painted, and the poet, whose wig and beard were made of rope. We literally used dyed hemp for his hair, hand laying each strand.

We had a lot of fun doing the juggler, who wore a nose piece, and had ears that wrapped around his head—an idea I've had for a long time. For a more whimsical look, we added spiked hair and eyebrows that grew up the center of his forehead.

My favorite character was the Wind Dancer, whose head was made of one-inch squares, painted yellow, red, orange and blue. His harlequin-like makeup consisted of a one-piece, pre-painted mask that covered most of his face, and each square had little separations between them to

create a three-dimensional look. We hired an actor who had the perfect face to animate the character, and he had a great time doing it. The visual effects department used opticals to enclose his head in a bubble that floated around until Worf bursts it later in the story.

Thanks to the Holodeck, I never know what sort of characters I'll be called upon to create. With an unlimited number of places and times to choose from, each story brings a new world of imagination to explore. ●

to devise a group of strange, whimsical characters that inhabited an alien artists' colony. There was the fire sculptor, who had an elaborate set of head appliances, the dancer, whose entire body

The Romulans

The Romulans returned in "The Neutral Zone"; their makeup gives them a built-in sullen expression.

There were a number of challenges we faced in bringing back the Romulans, the warlike race of aliens who had been part of the *STAR TREK* universe for more than two decades, and early on, became the main villains of *THE NEXT GENERATION*. First, we had to devise a makeup that was new and interesting, while staying true to some of the concepts introduced in the original series. Secondly, we had to come up with a way of making them more menacing. From the very first moment they appeared on screen, the viewer had to take them seriously, rather than seeing them as stereotyped villains with pointed ears. Finally, we wanted the Romulans to be markedly different from their mirror race, the Vulcans. The Vulcans were a wise, very passive civilization, and the Romulans were more warlike, aggressive and generally nastier. While the two races were completely different on a cultural level, it wasn't that easy to tell them apart physically. They had the same basic skin color, they wore the same hairstyle, and both races had pointed ears and arch-less eyebrows. Aside from dressing them up in different clothes, what were we going to do to bring out the diversity between them? That's when I came up with the forehead concept, which solved all three of our major problems with one simple but visually exciting solution.

I devised a forehead for the Romulans that had a dip in the center, and then I hollowed out the temple area. We wanted to stay close to their natural forehead, not making them look Ne-

The average Romulan makeup takes two hours to apply; half of that is spent gluing on the forehead and the ears.

Tomalak (Andreas Katsulas) is one of the the recurring Romulans in "Future Imperfect."

We tried to give the Romulan women a slightly different look from the men. Starting with Carolyn Seymour, who played a Romulan commander in "Contagion," I sculpted her forehead slightly "softer"; she had the same frowning look, but without the same boniness around the skull region that the male Romulans have.

With an older Romulan, I add a few more wrinkles to the forehead and the ears, so that they will blend in with the rest of the face. That's something that will frustrate you with any appliance. If the texture of the piece doesn't match up with the exposed areas

anderthal, not giving them a built-in sullen expression they couldn't get away from. Even if you saw a Romulan smile, you still wouldn't trust him.

Unlike the Klingons, I didn't fall into the trap of having to make a new forehead piece every time we had a Romulan guest star. Over the last five years, I've developed a series of about 10 different forehead designs, enough to fit almost any actor who comes in. There are a few designs that are a little bonier perhaps, and sometimes I'll try to bring the pitch of the frown into it a little more. Again, from a makeup standpoint, it was important that *no* two Romulans looked exactly alike.

Picard As Romulan

For me, the fascinating part of this was I had to wear a Romulan wig. I have a whole sequence of photographs taken of me with the makeup but without the wig, and I looked like one of those medieval gargoyles. I thought the Romulan look was incredibly successful, and the interesting thing was how much it helped to create a slightly different personality. It was quite a brilliant makeup."

—Patrick Stewart

Denise Crosby's appearance did not change significantly when she returned as Tasha Yar's daughter Sela.

look of the Vulcans. That's one of the reasons I originally designed the forehead with a V frown in it: to pick up the shape of the widow's peak. With the advent of new hairstylists on the show, the size of the widow's peak has sometimes been diminished.

I feel that there are certain things that we have to stay true to on *THE NEXT GENERATION*, especially when it's something that's already been established in

of the face, it destroys the illusion. of makeup artists just go for the design and forget about its integration; that's why so many good ideas turn out poorly once they've been applied. On *THE NEXT GENERATION*, we try to carry our ideas to their logical conclusion. If we're doing an elderly Romulan, such as Mimi Cozzens, who played the soup woman in "Unification," I make sure the forehead and face blend seamlessly together, just as I would with an old-age makeup on a human being.

The other major change I made with the Romulans was to give their hair a little widow's peak, as opposed to the very soft bang

Geordi is subjected to Romulan brainwashing techniques in "The Mind's Eye."

a previous story. There are viewers who watch these episodes a number of times, and notice these differences. Besides, as far as the Romulans are concerned, it's kind of fun to stay historically true to some of the ideas that Fred Phillips and my aunt (who worked as the hairstylist on the original series) established 25 years ago.

Getting back to the idea of skin color, we use the same makeup

Sela helps foment a Klingon/Romulan plot in "Redemption II."

Photo by Robbie Robinson: ©1992 Paramount Pictures

base on both the Vulcans and the Romulans—the makeup color is called LN-1, which literally stands for Leonard Nimoy. It's a very light yellow base. Again, just as I do with the Klingons who are made up with varying shades of brown, I try not to make all our Romulans the same shade of yellow. LN-1 is the main foundation color, so I use different shades of green and yellow to do highlighting and shadow, so it doesn't look exactly like the color of another Romulan in the same episode.

The average Romulan makeup takes about two hours to apply. Half of that is devoted to gluing on the forehead piece and the ears, and then another 30 minutes to put on the rest of the makeup. They've also got to get their wigs and eyebrows applied, and the

Data As Romulan

It was a piece of cake to play a Romulan, because it was just makeup. I didn't have to wear my contacts, which was particularly nice. To me, one of the worst parts of Data's makeup is the contacts. Even though they're my own prescription and just happen to be painted yellow, I just couldn't wear them for 15 hours every day. When I played a Romulan, they used my own eyes, so I didn't have to wear contacts, and that was a blessing. I think that I looked a little bit like the Keebler Elf!"

—*Brent Spiner*

Photo by Robbie Robinson: ©1992 Paramount Pictures

Photo by Michael Leshnov: ©1992 Paramount Pictures

Vulcan ambassador T'Pel turns out to be a Romulan spy in "Data's Day."

yellow Romulan body makeup has to be sponged onto their hands and neck.

Whenever we bring back a Romulan who has been in a previous episode, I'll request a black-and-white photograph or a clip from the old show as reference. If I've custom-made a forehead and/or ears for him in the past, I'll make new ones so everything will match perfectly.

Because the Romulans are such an aggressive species, several episodes have called for us to create characters that are wounded or dying. It started in the third season with "The Enemy," which had a dying Romulan brought aboard the *Enterprise*, as well as his shipmate who was stranded on the planet's surface with Geordi. A few weeks later, we did "The Defector," where we had to make up a badly-injured James Sloyan, whose character was trying to defect from the Romulan empire. In both cases, we used green blood for their wounds, an old *STAR TREK* idea that has been used many times. Since the Vulcans and Romulans are descended from the same race we reasoned, they would both have the same green blood.

We also established in "The Defector" that Romulans had an accelerated metabolism that enabled their wounds to heal quickly. I think they threw a line into the script somewhere because they didn't want any of our Romulan characters walking around with large wounds for an entire episode. I would design the facial appliances to show that fast healing ability, but sometimes an intermediary scene would be cut out and it would look like the wounds healed instantly.

"The Next Phase" Photo by Robbie Robinson; ©1992 Paramount Pictures

Varel (Susanna Thompson) and Mirok (Thomas Kopache) are two of the latest Romulan villains in "The Next Phase."

Gelatin was used to create the severe burn makeup seen in the opening sequence of "The Next Phase."

Lighting enhances the look of sullen power on Varel's face.

More recently, we had to create a severe burn makeup in "The Next Phase," for a scene where the bridge of a Romulan ship has been devastated by an explosion. As the camera pans across the set, we had a close-up of a badly-burned Romulan in the foreground; in most cases, the shot doesn't dwell for long on a single character, so if someone has to be injured or dead, the wounds have to be visible enough so they'll read to the audience. In this case, we used gelatin to simulate the burns, making them large and more obvious.

We've had some wonderful Romulans on the show. Carolyn Seymour, whom I mentioned earlier, played her character really mean and nasty, and I thought she did a great job. Of course there was Andreas Katsulas, who played Tomalak, one of our recurring Romulans, Malachi Throne, who was very memorable as Senator Pardek in "Unification," and Norman Large, who took time out from his work in the musical, *Phantom of the Opera*, and appeared in "Unification."

Probably one of our most thought-provoking Romulan makeups was done for Denise Crosby, who returned to the series as Sela, the daughter of Tasha Yar. Even though Denise's character was supposed to be half-human/half-Romulan, the producers wanted her to look more human. We gave her a small pair of ear tips, but that was our only concession to her Romulan heritage. We didn't put the stylized forehead piece on her or change her eyebrows, but the hairstyle that was selected for her managed to cover most of that anyway. They selected the wig

after several hair tests, and I think it worked out beautifully for our purposes.

I think the reason for wanting Denise to look more human was the need for instant recognition from the viewers. They didn't want us to alter her appearance so much that you'd say, "Oh, is *that* Denise?" By leaving her face alone, changing the hairstyle, and putting the ear tips on her, it was enough of a change where you could say, "That's Denise, but she has pointed ears, so she must be half-Romulan."

Many people have wondered if that was actually Denise standing in the shadows for "The Mind's Eye," the story that paved the way for her return in "Redemption." That *was* her in those scenes where you hear her voice, but we knew ahead of time that she wouldn't be seen, so we didn't have to make her up.

Two of our other cast members who became Romulans for a couple of episodes were Patrick Stewart and Brent Spiner, in "Unification." For the scenes where Picard and Data had to disguise themselves to infiltrate the planet Romulus, we found a pair of ears to fit each of them, gave them the pointed eyebrows, and applied Romulan-style foreheads. Since Brent and Patrick both have high foreheads to begin with, I think that helped make their makeup even more convincing.

I remember not long after "Unification," Patrick auctioned off a pair of his Romulan ears to raise money for Amnesty International. He used to collect his ears every day to do that.

Looking back at the number of Romulan stories we've done over the last five seasons of *THE NEXT GENERATION*, it's nice to know that we've had a small part in their success and development. Whenever our viewers see the Romulans in a new episode, they're never sure if they can be trusted, as we've seen in stories like "Future Imperfect" and "The Next Phase." I'd like to think that the evil, frowning look I've created for them may have something to do with it. ●

Aging Effects

Step-by-Step Aging FX for Brent Spiner in "Brothers."

O ne of the most exciting aspects of working on *THE NEXT GENERATION* is having to come up with complicated makeup effects within a relatively short period of time. While it would be nice to conduct extensive makeup tests as we do on feature films, there are more restrictions working on a weekly TV series, and when you do something like an elaborate aging makeup, it has to work the first time.

I've always found aging effects to be a tremendous challenge for a makeup artist, because they have to be based on reality. If I'm creating a futuristic alien or a prehistoric man, I can get away with a little more, because the audience doesn't necessarily know what I'm trying to accomplish. If I'm aging a well-known actor into a 90-year-old man, however, it has to look "real," or the audience will notice it right away; witness the negative reaction to some of the films and TV programs that used aging makeups unsuccessfully for proof of that.

Sometimes the best aging makeup is one you never notice. One of my Oscar nominations and nearly half my Emmy nominations are for old-age makeups, but some of my best work has gone virtually unnoticed because of its subtlety. I did a film years ago called *True Confessions*, in which I spent four hours aging Robert DeNiro. The makeup had a few small appliances around the eyes, but the rest was done subtly, using a bald cap and wig, individually placing grey hairs into the eyebrows, and stretching rubber around the eyes to suggest

"In this case, it was a limited situation. I only had to go into that makeup three times on three different days. It was a three-hour makeup, but the effect was so tremendous, and it was such a brilliant design, that what it gave me in terms of how to play it was invaluable. Looking at this man in the mirror who was not me, I had a better understanding of who he was than I did internally at that point.

"Also, people started treating me like I was old, even though I had worked with them for three years at that point. Everybody was treating me with so much more respect, because I was a man who had lived a long life, and I deserved special treatment. It was really interesting to see that, and the older I acted between scenes, the nicer people treated me. It was incredible."

—*Brent Spiner*

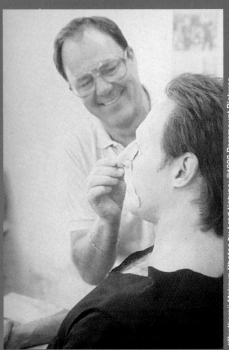

"Brothers" Makeup Photos by Fred Sabine: ©1992 Paramount Pictures

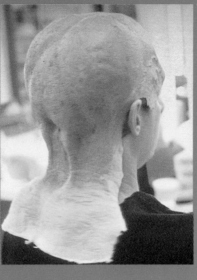

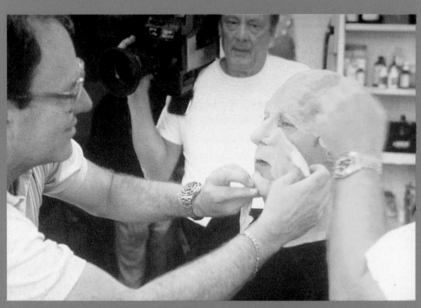

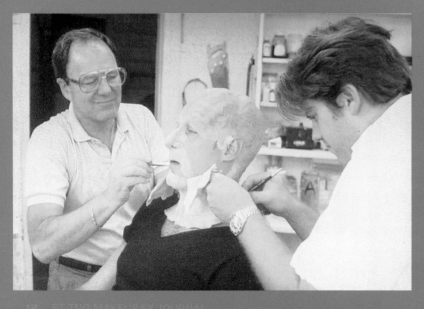

wrinkles. The makeup was largely ignored, which I actually took to be a great compliment. It meant I was doing my job right. My Uncle Perc once said, "The best compliment to a great makeup is no compliment at all."

Over the last five years, we've done some interesting aging effects on THE NEXT GENERATION. The early ones might have been a little simple because they had to be done so quickly, but as time went on, they became more complex. By the time we got to the fifth season, I think the makeup we did on Patrick Stewart for "The Inner Light" was as good as anything ever done for a feature film. It was just a matter of learning what could be done within the time that was available.

Our first aging makeup was done for the pilot, "Encounter at Farpoint," which featured a cameo appearance by DeForest Kelley, playing a very old Admiral McCoy. The production team didn't want us to do any elaborate work on DeForest; just some wrinkles and a white wig. The only appliance we used on his face was a forehead piece, and even that wasn't made specifically for him. For the rest of DeForest's face, we stretched the skin and applied latex to it, creating wrinkles.

If I had that makeup to do over again, I would take a cast of De-Forest's head and create a few new pieces. If I had time to create an appliance to make the throat look older, or even make a different forehead piece, the overall makeup design would have been improved dramatically.

A few months later, we had our first chance to do an extensive aging makeup, for "Too Short a Season." The script called for Admiral Jameson (played by Clayton Rohner) to start the episode as a 70 or 80-year-old-man. As a result of taking an experimental youth drug, he continued to get younger and younger as the story goes on. I think there were about three or four stages needed to bring Clayton back to his actual youthful appearance. We had to go through the entire script, blocking it out and deciding where each change should take place.

The first stage was the most complex, requiring a large number of appliances to turn Clayton into the 80-year-old Jameson. There was a bald cap, a forehead, eyepieces for the upper and lower part of the eye, a throat piece, jowls and a wig. The makeup took four hours to apply.

It was while we were doing the 80-year-old Jameson that I learned a valuable lesson about handling stress. There was only Werner Keppler and myself doing the show at that time, and I was doing so much of the work, that one day I walked out the makeup trailer and literally stood there, unable to move. I was so exhausted that the studio had to send me home with a driver.

The next morning, I was supposed to stay in bed, but I knew we were doing the 80-year-old Jameson makeup, and I was worried about how it would turn out. I showed up at the studio a few hours later than usual, and the makeup was already way behind schedule. We had slated four hours to work on Clayton, and when I walked in after three hours, it was only half done. I had to pitch in to help finish the job on time, and after that, I learned to start pacing myself a bit more. It's very easy to get burned out on a work-intensive show like *THE NEXT GENERATION* if you're not careful.

Looking back at the Admiral Jameson makeup, I suppose I was happy with it under the circumstances. If you're doing an old age makeup on a youthful face, you have to completely cover the face in some way to create the illusion of age. If part of the actor's young face comes through, it destroys the effect.

Again, it all comes down to having enough time. If I was working on a film, and had several months to test Clayton's makeup beforehand, it probably would have turned out more to my liking. With less than a week to work with, I don't think it turned out too badly.

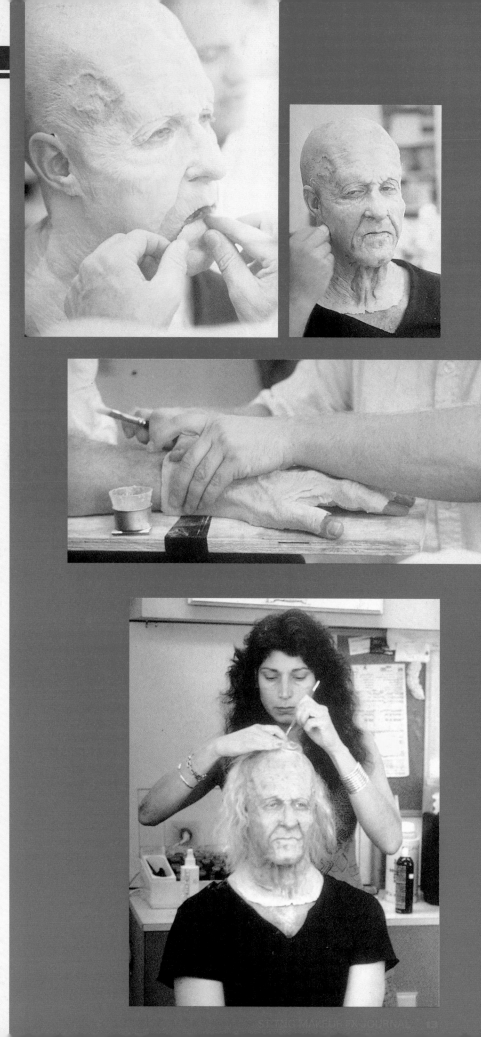

By the second season, we had managed to establish a certain rhythm on the series, and when a script arrived, everyone had much more confidence and control over what we were doing. For those reasons, Diana Muldaur's aging makeup in "Unnatural Selection" turned out much better than the work we had done for "Too Short a Season."

The story called for Dr. Pulaski to catch a rare disease, which caused her to age rapidly. Our task was made easier by the fact that Diana had a more mature face, and we were able to make intermediate changes by using highlight, shadow and a little stretch rubber. The problem we had with Clayton Rohner the previous season was that his face was so young that it was impossible to make those changes without using appliances.

For the final stages of Diana's makeup, we made a cast of her face and created a set of appliances that would fit her. Overall, I was happy with the end result; it was the best aging makeup we had done for the series up to that point.

During our third season, I got to do an interesting aging makeup on Patrick Stewart in "The Defector," for the Holodeck scene where Data and Picard are performing Shakespeare's *Henry V*. I enjoyed that one. It was a nice combination of character and aging.

I should point out that creating a successful aging effect does not necessarily mean covering an actor's face with rubber. Sometimes the subtle approach is called for, as in "Future Imperfect," where each member of the cast had to age 16 years. The producers decided that rather than having each actor sit in a makeup chair for two or three hours, it would be a better idea to suggest their age by changing the hairstyles, and maybe doing a little rubber stretching around the eyes. I thought it was a sensible approach, because most of our actors were in their 30s, and even aging them 16 years would only put them in their mid-40s. Most

Michael Westmore took advantage of Diana Muldaur's natural facial features to create some very subtle makeup FX.

people don't look dramatically different at that age, and it would have been a waste of time and energy using prosthetics to achieve that effect.

If I had to choose my favorite aging makeup from *THE NEXT GENERATION,* I would have a difficult time deciding between Brent Spiner's Dr. Soong makeup in "Brothers," and more recently, the work we did with Patrick Stewart in "The Inner Light." It would be difficult to pick one over the other, because they both worked very well within their respective stories, and from a technical standpoint, there's very little I would change about either one. I feel the same way about them as I did about *2010*, where my work on Keir Dullea earned an Oscar nomination.

I think that "Brothers" was one of our finest episodes, not only for the memorable aging effects we created (which were nominated for an Emmy in 1991) but also for Brent's acting *tour de force*, playing Data, Lore *and* Dr. Soong. I think it was the first time an actor ever played three different characters on camera like that, and it's a shame that his brilliant performance didn't receive more recognition.

The first thing I did in creating Brent's makeup for Dr. Soong, was build up his cranial structure, to suggest that he had more brain cells than a normal human being. In addition, we then did a full

Diana Muldaur's aging makeup in "Unnatural Selection," was acclaimed as one of the best for the series at that time.

"Unnatural Selection" Photo: ©1992 Paramount Pictures

Patrick Stewart on "The Inner Light"

"The interesting thing in terms of the acting was finding out how this man would have developed had his circumstances been different. I thought quite carefully about how I would sound, how I would move, how a man's manner would change when he has spent 30 years not being the principal authority figure. He was just a private individual, living quietly with his family.

"I was very much in the hands of Michael, June Haymore and Doug Drexler; Michael designed the makeup, and June and Doug were mostly responsible for applying it. The only contribution I made to that was suggesting that the first aging should simply be a lengthening of my own hair. Since something like five years had gone by, I had a hairpiece that made my own hair a little longer, a little more unkempt, and a little stragglier, which immediately suggests that this is not the Picard we saw minutes ago. Long hair always makes me look older, so this was a very significant phase in the aging.

"The older the makeup got, the more I looked at it in the mirror and found that it began to affect me physically and mentally, a slowing-down process. Leaving the makeup trailer, I would find myself stepping carefully down from it, and the makeup encouraged me to stay within that all day long.

"By the time I reached my maximum aging, there was barely any of my own skin visible. It was all latex by then. The thing you have to rely on more than any other time are the eyes and the voice to communicate, because no matter how brilliant the latex is, it's not living tissue.

"I loved watching that makeup be-ing put on. I meditate, and because it took four to five hours to put on the major makeup, I would do a meditation in the middle of it, so when I came out of it having had my eyes closed, there were sometimes major changes that had taken place. Some of my deepest meditations took place in the makeup chair; in fact, they told me at one point they had to stop doing part of the makeup because my head had become so relaxed that they had to wait until I came around.

"The makeup was an enormous asset, although I didn't look at myself much when it was on, because it looked so odd. Of course, what inevitably happened was I found myself looking like my father, who's been dead for 10 years now, and that was a somewhat unnerving aspect of it.

"The most affecting sequence was the one scene where I was with the actress who was playing my wife, late one warm evening, sitting on a bench outside. I remember looking at her at one point and thinking, 'This is what it feels like to be elderly: sitting on a bench with someone you know so well, and this is what lies ahead.' That was the one time I had a sense of, God willing, what was waiting for me."

—Patrick Stewart

four-hour aging makeup on him. We had special contacts made for his eyes to simulate cataracts, I made an old-looking set of teeth to cover his real teeth, and we covered his entire face with a thin layer of appliances. We even made pieces to cover the backs of his hands.

From a technical standpoint, "Brothers" was a very difficult story to do, because of the trick photography needed to put three characters, all played by Brent, into the same shot. It took a day or so longer to shoot than an average episode, because each scene had to be re-shot three times, to include Data, Lore and Dr. Soong. Some shots required even more ingenuity—for a scene where Dr. Soong touches Data's face for example, we had to apply Brent's makeup on the back of somebody else's hand so it could appear in the same frame.

Fortunately for Brent, he only had to play one character at a time, so he didn't have to shift mental gears every few hours. It certainly made things easier for

A subtle approach to aging was tried on Picard and Troi in "Future Imperfect."

us as far as makeup changes were concerned.

My other favorite aging makeup was done for "The Inner Light," one of the final episodes of the fifth season. It was a wonderfully sensitive story, and I think Patrick Stewart gave one of his most moving performances as a quiet family man, trying to pass the memories of his dying civilization on to Picard.

Instead of having to do a single makeup as we did in "Brothers," this story called for Patrick's character to age slowly by 40 to 50 years. There were four or five intermediate stages involved, each one more complex than the last. For the first stage where only a few years had passed, we did a bit of shadowing under Patrick's eyes, then for the second, a bit of stippling, and for the final three stages, we used an increasing number of appliances. We also let his hair get progressively longer, and had special wigs made up for the final stages.

For Patrick's final makeup, we spent three or four hours putting appliances on him. Although we left the top of his head alone, we added pieces to his upper and lower eyes, his nose, ear lobes, throat, jowls, and the backs of his hands.

Patrick Stewart performed scenes from Shakespeare's *Henry V* in "The Defector"; his makeup demonstrates a good combination of specific character and aging.

Director Les Landau on "Future Imperfect"

"Initially, my reaction was that they should be obviously aged enough for the audience to realize that they look different, but not so aged that they should say, 'Oh boy, they're wearing a lot of makeup!' Once again, Michael was able to achieve with his concept of makeup and hairstyling a look that immediately lets the audience say, 'Hey, wait a minute, there's something different here; what is it?' When Riker first looks in that mirror in Sick Bay and sees the wrinkles, the sagging eyes and the grey hair, I think the audience is just as surprised as he is."

—Les Landau

Although a large part of our time on "The Inner Light" was spent developing the different stages of Patrick's makeup, we also had to age some of the other characters in the story. Margot Rose, who played Patrick's wife, started out in her mid-30s, and ended up at age 65. There were other actors who required less work, either using a few appliances or adding and removing hairpieces to suggest greater age.

Looking at that makeup now, I think it was easily as good as anything I've ever done, even for feature films. It might have been submitted for Emmy consideration, but because of the story's airdate, we missed the deadline by a single day. While it would have been nice to see the story get the recognition it deserved, I still think it looked fantastic.

While it's hard to imagine doing better aging makeup than "Brothers" or "The Inner Light," each story presents a new challenge, and a new person to work on. When you actually sit down with an actor and look at his features, you start to come up with ideas that never occurred to you before. There's no telling what we may come up with in the future.

It might be nice to further study some pictures of older people, and spend extra time trying to see how the muscles start to sag in certain areas of the face, or how a wrinkle might start to fold and develop. I'm not sure what my next aging makeup will look like, but the important thing is trying to make each one a little different, and more realistic than the last. ●

The Bolian:
Step-by-Step

Actor Leonard Jones gets ready for the makeup that will transform him into a Bolian for "Time's Arrow II."

We start by gluing on the appliance that will "split" the face in half.

Once the appliance has been glued in place, PAX paint is applied to give the face its basic blue color.

Dark blue shadows are added to the blue base, giving the makeup a more three-dimensional look.

Yellow highlights are added.

And there you have it: A genuine Bolian!

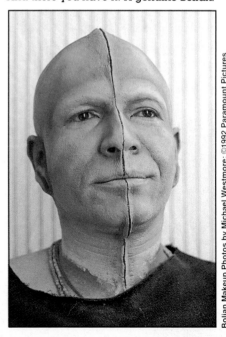

Humanoids & Aliens

If I had to sit down and compose a list of every humanoid race and alien being we've created for *THE NEXT GENERATION,* I would need an extremely long piece of paper, and a much better memory. While it's virtually impossible to discuss every single one of our alien makeups, there are a number of characters worth noting. Some of them have been seen in several episodes, while others have only been used once. A few have been photographed in long, lingering close-ups, and others, only fleetingly seen in the background of different scenes.

In discussing some of our lesser aliens and humanoids, I've tried to keep them in chronological order, starting with our oldest creations, and finishing with some of the characters seen in some of our most recent episodes. It's interesting to follow our progress through the first five seasons of *THE NEXT GENERATION,* and see how our creations have gotten more complex and exciting, as we started to realize what could be done. It makes me wonder what sort of characters we'll be creating in the years to come.

The Traveler

Many of our viewers don't know that Eric Menyuk, who played the Traveler, was on the studio's final list to play Data; it actually came down to a choice between Spiner and Eric. As it turned out, Spiner was chosen for the role, but the producers still kept Eric in mind. A few months later, when they needed an actor to play The Traveler, a mysterious dimension-hopping humanoid

Eric Menyuk, who played The Traveler, was also one of the studio's early possibilities to play Data.

who appeared in our fifth episode, "Where No One Has Gone Before," they called, and asked him to play the part.

Eric's Traveler makeup consisted mainly of a forehead piece that ran into his hairline and down onto his nose. I also created a pair of large, three-fingered hands for him, making him a little different from a normal human being. We were still early in our first season, and really hadn't started to explore what we could do with elaborate humanoid makeups.

The Traveler turned out to be popular enough to warrant his return in the fourth-season story, "Remember Me." There was no reason to make any appliance changes, but I did make his face more opalescent.

"Where No One Has Gone Before" Photo: ©1988 Paramount Pictures

An alien musician was created for "Menage a Troi."

Photo by Robbie Robinson: ©1991 Paramount Pictures

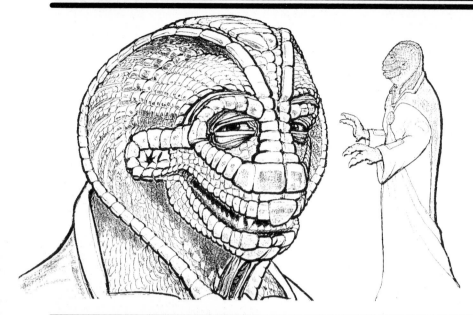

the other three. The background actors who had to wear them were very uncomfortable. I still have those heads in my lab, and if you dropped one, instead of bouncing, it would probably put a hole in the floor.

Looking back at those masks, I'm still happy with both of them. Although the Dog heads didn't allow for any movement, we did have a close-up where one of the actors was able to stick his tongue between the jaws and teeth of the mask, making it look "alive."

If I was remaking the Snake heads today, I would certainly make them much lighter, and find a way to create more movement in them. In a recent episode, where we used a Selay in Ten-Forward, I used intense highlighting and shading on the scales to give the mask a three-dimensional look.

The Bynars

The original concept for the Bynars, which appeared in "11001001," was a race of small creatures which didn't speak, but had another method of communicating with each other. We

Michael Westmore created these Selay heads for "Lonely Among Us."

A last-minute casting change forced Westmore to completely redesign the makeup for Palor Toff (Nehemiah Persoff) in "The Most Toys."

The Anticans and The Selay

In addition to the Traveler, "Lonely Among Us" also featured two races of feuding aliens, called the Anticans and the Selay, or "the Snakes and the Dogs," as we were fond of calling them. We had to make head masks and hands for both groups of creatures, (there were two Dogs and five of the Snakes). From start to finish, the Dogs were created in our Paramount lab, but the Snakes were made in a different lab. I had to keep running over there to

check on the progress. Once the head was sculptured, they made a mold of it and sent me the unpainted latex pieces to finish.

A problem we had with the Snake heads was that I wanted them cast from a lightweight four-pound polyurethane that would be flexible enough. For some reason, the heads came out as heavy and rigid as rocks; they weren't soft and pliable at all. I was able to re-cast the two principal Snake heads at the last minute, with a soft foam rubber, but because those masks took five hours to cook, there was no time to redo

wanted them small, but couldn't use children without bringing in teachers, and worrying about the number of hours the kids could work each day. The solution was to hire a group of young women who were short and had a pretty, childlike aura. They would work in pairs, with the device facing each other, making it look as if they were electronically "connected." The women had a battery pack mounted to their waists, allowing them to control the device. The blinking made it look as though they were communicating with each other.

Their makeup consisted of a large appliance which fitted the head like a bathing cap, coming down across the bridge of the nose, over the cheekbones and around the neck. The ears were asymmetrical, to reinforce the connection between each pair of women. We decided to make them a light purplish color, which blended nicely with the neutral look of the costumes.

A problem we had with the makeup was that each headpiece was created from the same mold, and had to be cut and trimmed to fit each of the women. That's the reason for putting a little bit of

The Bynars were played by a group of young women, who worked in pairs, making it look as if they were electronically connected.

purple hair on the side of the neck: It was used to hide a join line.

The Bynars turned out very well, and I think we can do more with them if they ever return.

The Benzites

If I was making a list of characters I'd like to bring back in a future NEXT GENERATION episode, the Benzites would be one of my first choices. We've only used them twice, but with all the improvements we've made in the series over the last five years, I'd love to take another crack at them.

Our first Benzite character was Mordock, who appeared in "Coming of Age"; one of the cadets competing with Wesley in the Starfleet entrance exam. The script originally called for an alien who wore a vapor breathing apparatus, and that was the entire description I was given.

The makeup I created for actor John Putch was one of the most elaborate designs created for the first season. We had one piece which covered most of the head, and additional pieces for the up-

per lip, chin and eyelids. I made a special set of eyelids for John, using a trick I had once used on Roddy McDowall for the Remo Williams television pilot. Instead of creating oriental eyes however, I was able to devise a pair of puffy eyes with thin lids that folded into themselves like a set of venetian blinds.

There was also a set of catfish-like feelers around the mouth area, and another set of tendrils hanging from each earlobe which had been added by my daughter. I was sculpting the head at home over the Christmas break, and it was sitting on the dining room table. McKenzie walked in, picked up a little blob of clay in her hand and said, "Why don't you put something here?" and added the small feelers to the bottom of the ear lobes. I thought they were a nice touch and left them on.

I decided to make the headpiece a blue color, simply because we hadn't done a blue alien yet. I also worked yellows and oranges into the color scheme to make the skin more interesting and life-like.

We had a scene where Mordock was working on a computer, and his hands would

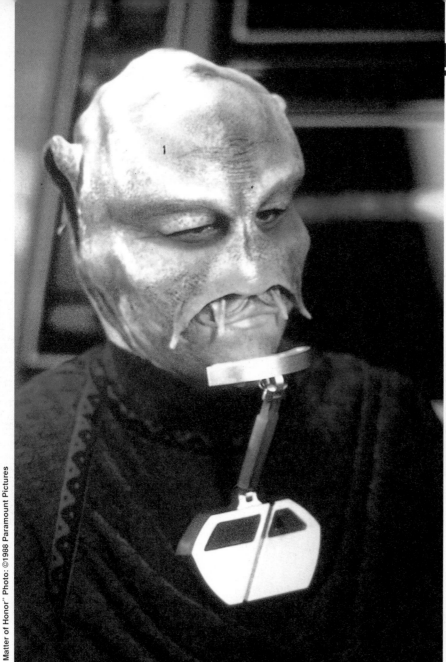

The makeup created for Mendon (John Putch) was one of the most elaborate designs done in the first season.

to be able to get to him if he had trouble breathing. The mouth was created with three holes in it, so if we had to, we could stick our fingers right inside the mask and clean the gunk out of his mouth in a hurry.

Once wardrobe dressed the stuntman in his suit and we put the mask on him, he stood on a grate and was lowered into the oil. Since there wasn't a breathing apparatus in the suit, the man had to hold his breath. While he was under, we had to time the scene with a stopwatch. In retrospect, it probably would have been a good idea to build a small oxygen tank into the head so we didn't have to worry as much.

The one problem with the suit was that it kept reacting with the oil. That goo was actually a water soluble methocel material, dyed with water-based black printer's ink to look like oil. It was supposed to be inert, but for some reason we've never been able to explain, the suit would start to disintegrate by the end of the day. It never bothered the

be featured. I created an opposable thumb that slipped over his little finger, so when we see his hands, he has three fingers and two thumbs. It added time to the makeup, but the effect was well worth it.

When we brought John back in the second season for "A Matter of Honor," he played another Benzite called Mendon, who looked identical to his predecessor. It meant that we were able to use the same mold again, but this time, I tried to brighten up the colors. That was before I learned how to use an airbrush, so everything was still hand-painted. I'd love to bring the character back now, because I could do it a lot faster and make it more colorful.

Armus

The idea behind Armus, the oil slick monster created for "Skin of Evil," was to design a being that could rise out of a pit of oil, and the Away Team would be unable to reason with it or affect it.

The makeup chores for Armus were divided between my department, which designed the head, and an outside company which built the body. By that time, we had hired Gerald Quist as an additional makeup artist, and the two of us spent an entire day sculpting the head together.

One thing we were aware of while we were designing the head was that the stuntman who would wear it would have to go down into a pit of black goo, and we had

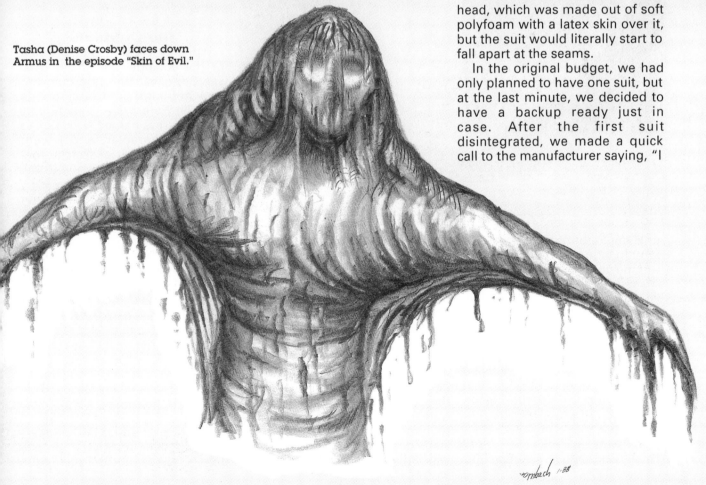

Tasha (Denise Crosby) faces down Armus in the episode "Skin of Evil."

head, which was made out of soft polyfoam with a latex skin over it, but the suit would literally start to fall apart at the seams.

In the original budget, we had only planned to have one suit, but at the last minute, we decided to have a backup ready just in case. After the first suit disintegrated, we made a quick call to the manufacturer saying, "I

Mr. Mot, the ship's barber, is a Bolian.

The Bolians

We've used the Bolians a number of times on THE NEXT GENERATION, particularly Mr. Mot, the blue barber who keeps popping up on the Enterprise. He's a fun character to bring back, and an interesting reminder to our viewers that there are many different races on the ship.

Our first Bolian character was Michael Berryman, who played Captain Rixx in "Conspiracy." His makeup consisted of a series of raised appliances that made his face look as if it was split down the middle. The pieces ran up the back of his neck, over the top of his head, down his face and all the way down his throat. I colored his face a light blue, which unfortunately was difficult to see because of the red lighting used in that scene. We've used different shades of blue on the Bolians since then, including the girl captured with Picard in "Allegiance," and of course, the barber.

The Dremans

We only created one Dreman for the episode "Pen Pals;" that was Sarjenka, the little girl who Data befriends and later brings onto the Enterprise. They hired a young actress named Nikki Cox to play the character, and I went through a number of sketches before we finally came up with the selected design. Most of my early ideas had antennae on them, but those were eliminated. I finally came up with a design which consisted of a slip-on headpiece and a red, spiky wig. We then added gold glitter to her orange skin and hair to give them a metallic sheen. I also made long finger extensions for her, which were made out of clear plastic and fitted over her own fingers. Because the extensions were translucent, the light would shine through them when she held up her hands, producing a wonderful effect.

When Nikki got to the set however, the director of photography didn't realize her fingers were

think you'd better make a few more!" During the four days we used the suits, every one of them fell apart.

If we were filming those scenes today, we could get much better results by using opticals, in conjunction with a man in a suit. Everyone was thrilled with it back then, but so much has happened with optical effects over the last few years that we could probably come up with more effective visuals today.

There was also a scene in "Skin of Evil" where Riker is pulled into the pool of oil, and a few minutes later, we see his face slowly emerge from the goo. The guy who actually got dragged into the pit was a stuntman dressed in Riker's Starfleet uniform. For the second part of the scene, I built a plaster cast of Jonathan's head with the mouth open and painted it black. The head was laid on the platform and slowly raised out of the pool. The oily black goo was tremendously messy, and we had to hook up a hose outside the stage door to rinse it off. Everyone was filthy with the stuff.

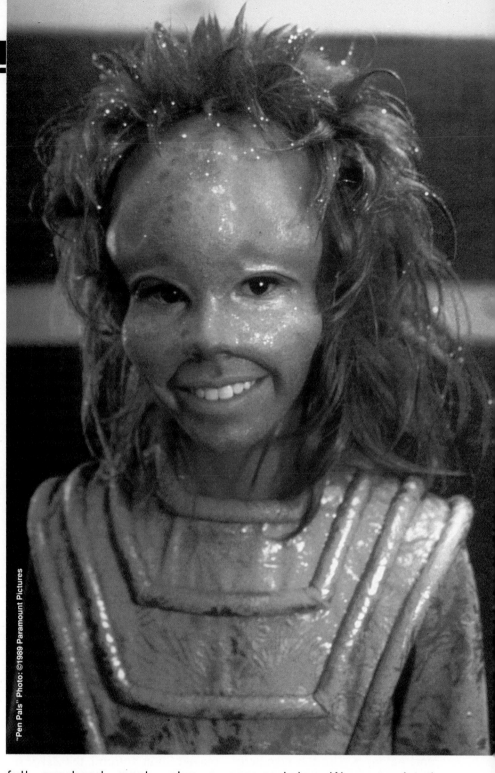

"Pen Pals" Photo: ©1989 Paramount Pictures

supposed to be clear. He called
me and said, "Put some makeup
on her fingers; I can see through
them!" I replied that they were
supposed to be that way, there
was a pause, and then he said,
"OK." Unfortunately, the effect
was never really focused upon.

The Pakleds

Somebody once referred to the
Pakleds as "the sharpei people;"
they almost looked like those cute
little dogs you see, that have a
sad, helpless look, and rolls of
wrinkles that cover their faces.

We wanted to create a race of
humanoids that would look slow
and harmless, that weren't capa-
ble of creating their own technology and had to borrow it from
other cultures. You would want to
feel sorry for them and try to help
them out, but beneath the innocent exterior, they actually had a
very mean, sneaky streak. We
hired a group of large, portly actors that gave the characters a
Tweedledee/Tweedledum sort of
appearance, and I designed
whimsical faces to support that
concept. We added appliances to
their foreheads, cheeks and the
tips of their noses, and I designed
a set of eyebrows that went up to
the center of the forehead to give
them even more of a sad look. I
also made a large set of front
teeth which weren't noticeable,
but worked well with the overall
makeup. It was a successful
design. The early scenes where
the *Enterprise* meets the Pakleds,
for the first time, and Geordi's
later encounter with the creatures,
are still very funny.

The Antedians

One of the most unusual guest
stars we had during the early days
of *THE NEXT GENERATION* was
singer Mick Fleetwood, who
played one of the fishlike Antedians in "Manhunt." Mick loved
playing an alien, and even shaved
off the beard he had worn for 10
years so that we could make a
cast of his head.

For the two Antedians, I built a
full overhead mask, plus a
separate piece which covered the
lower lip, the chin and the front of
the throat. By making the mask in
two separate pieces, the actors
were able to open and close their
mouths, making the heads mov-
able.

Unfortunately, a lot of our work
on the heads went unnoticed due
to time limitations. Both masks
had eyes that could blink, and a
set of gills that had giant air bladders built into them. By blowing
into a set of air hoses off-camera,
we were able to make the gills
open and close. We even painted
the inside of the gills a shiny red
to look like a real fish.

There was one shot where the
Antedians are lying on a table after coming out of a coma, the
eyes suddenly blink open and
they start breathing. Because the
show was running too long, they
cut the scene right after the eyes
opened, and nobody got to see
the gills work.

The other effect that was never
really seen properly was the fin
that went down the center of each
head and the back of the hands.

The fins were made out of a clear urethane, and if a light shone through them, it would produce a glow. Early one morning, after making up Mick for the day's filming, we were walking down an alleyway just as the sun was coming up. Mick happened to turn sideways, and the sun came through the fin on top of his head. It looked gorgeous, but we didn't have the back lighting conditions to duplicate the effect on the set.

We had another funny scene where the two Antedians had to reach into a tub filled with something that looked like squid, and start eating it. The tub was actually filled with pieces of gelatin, and when the cameras started rolling, both actors got in there and really started shoveling it into their mouths. It was the best eating scene we had on the show since "Conspiracy," where one of the worms accidentally fell into Jonathan's mouth. We were going to use little rice crackers for the actual closeup, but Jonathan decided to use the live props. He held them right over his mouth, and one of those little guys got loose and fell in. I don't think he'll ever forget that scene!

"The Pakleds were supposed to be a race of what appeared to be an ugly and slow-thinking people," says director Les Landau of "Samaritan Snare." "We had to incorporate a visual look to them that would enhance that kind of race. Their looks were in total contrast to what they actually were."

The Zakdorns

Sometimes it's hard to design a humanoid makeup until we actually know who the actor is and what he looks like. A good example of this is Roy Brocksmith, who played Sima Kolrami, the Zakdorn strategist in "Peak Performance." There was nothing in the script telling me what the character would look like, and it wasn't until I started sculpting over the cast of Roy's head that I was able to come up with an idea.

Roy has a full, round face, and I designed a set of appliances that would work with his features. We made a piece that went over his nose and upper lip, two pieces for the cheeks and an appliance for his forehead. I didn't want to do anything with his hair, so the hair stylist slicked it back, exposing more of his face. I also left his hands alone, because I knew there would be several scenes of him playing a game, and he would need his hands free.

Once we had established what the Zakdorns looked like in "Peak Performance," I used the same makeup for the Zakdorn quartermaster in "Unification." It was just a matter of adjusting and making a new set of appliances to fit the actor.

The Caldonians

We had a character in the third-season story, "The Price," called Leyor of the Caldonians. He was played by the late Kevin Peter Hall, a very tall actor who also played the Predator and Harry in *Harry and the Hendersons.* The Caldonians were my first attempt

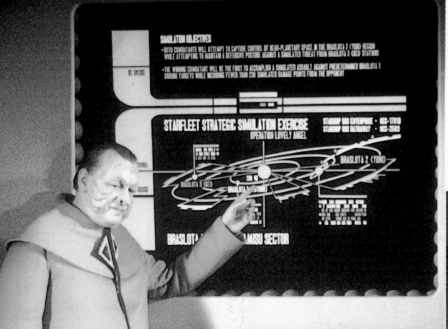

Opera House Head." We also had a Bolian character played by Joycelyn O'Brien, who wore the same split face appliances and blue coloring we had established with Michael Berryman in "Conspiracy." We colored her a very light blue, and added a blue lipstick for contrast.

to do something really elaborate with an alien forehead, as opposed to some of the simple humanoids we had been doing up to that point. We had another humanoid in that story, a Barzan woman who had a forehead appliance and purple tubes that went into the sides of her face, but Kevin was our big makeup. I spent a lot of time designing a large, extended forehead for him, which further emphasized his height, and we worked closely with the wardrobe department, who created a headdress that reduced the amount of rubber we had to use. Wardrobe also made a set of three-fingered gloves which changed the shape of Peter's hands. The overall design worked very well, and it set the stage for some of the more complicated work we'd be doing in the future.

"Allegiance" Aliens

I'm very proud of the makeup we did for "Allegiance," the third-season story which received an Emmy nomination in 1990. We had to create several characters for this episode, starting with Mr. Thal, a Myzerian played by Stephen Markle. Stephen had a wrinkled, striated face, almost like a villain from *Dick Tracy*, and he wore an elaborate hood which led us to nickname him "The Sydney

The idea for the Vorgon's scallopy crest came from a seashell.

A German actor named Reiner Schone played a beast-man from the planet Challna. His makeup was broken down into several different pieces, including two sets of protruding tusks, and special contact lenses which made his eyes red and yellow, more animal-like. The lenses could only be worn for a short period of time, and we had to have a technician standing by to remove them. Despite the uncomfortable makeup, Reiner had a great time playing the part, and really threw himself into it.

Rounding out our group of guest stars was a race of aliens who had abducted Picard and the others for observation. Jeff and Jerry Rector, a set of identical twins, were hired to play the creatures, which had large, lumpy yellowish heads with big nostrils. Both actors looked exactly alike in body shape, head size and facial features, so we were able to use a duplicate set of appliances on them.

The Vorgons

I originally got the idea for the Vorgons, the time-traveling aliens in "Captain's Holiday," from a sea shell. I designed their makeup to include a scallopy crest that ran up the face and all the way to the back of the head. There was one pre-painted headpiece, and additional pieces to cover the front of the face and throat. Once the appliances had been blended together, we matched up the color patterns using an airbrush. I also used an iridescent paint to give the heads a slight glow. The final makeup took almost four hours.

Once the heads were painted, I added a little electronic device to the side of each head. It was a pair of battery-powered earrings that my daughter had gotten for Christmas, that had a little computer pattern of constantly changing, abstract pictures. I thought the square earring device on the Vorgons suggested in a subtle way, that they were time-travelers from the future. There's only one

scene where you can really see them, when both characters are in profile.

The Malcorians

Most people now remember "First Contact" for the classic scene between Riker and a Malcorian named Lanel, who "always wanted to make love with an alien." We had a wonderful group of guest stars on that episode, including Bebe Neuwirth, who played Lanel, George Coe and Carolyn Seymour, who had previously appeared as a Romulan commander in "Contagion."

Because we were showing a race whose development ran parallel to 20th-Century Earth, we didn't want the Malcorians to look *too* alien. I designed a forehead piece to change their faces and a set of hands that weren't quite human-looking, but would perform the same functions. The fingers were webbed together, and had little suckers on the end that could be used to grip objects.

German actor Reiner Schone had a great time playing a beast-man `Esoqq from the planet Chalna.

"Allegiance" Photo: ©1992 Paramount Pictures

There was a little cap that covered the thumb, which also had a sucker on it.

"First Contact" was probably one of our better stories; in fact, I'd include it in a list of our top 20 episodes. We also had to turn Jonathan into a Malcorian, which was a lot of fun, and his scene with Bebe Neuwirth is one that

fans of the series will probably be talking about for years. Bebe really enjoyed coming over from *Cheers* to do that scene, and once she was in makeup, was able to get into her character. In fact, she had to go back to *Cheers* one afternoon to do a reading, and didn't want to get cleaned up. She just went over as a Malcorian.

"Identity Crisis"

I don't think too many people realize how much work went into creating the lizard creatures of "Identity Crisis." Not only did we have to transform LeVar Burton and Broadway actress Maryann Plunkett into the glowing aliens, but we also had to construct additional suits for the background characters who had already been transformed. The episode was nominated for an Emmy in 1991, but was probably overshadowed by "Brothers," which received more media attention.

The original concept in the script stated that if the Away Team stayed too long on the planet's surface, they would eventually contract a parasitic virus that would slowly change them into lizard-like creatures. In the first stages of the transformation, little blue veins began to appear on the neck and face, and the fingers start to grow together. Each vein was a tiny appliance that had to be glued on, and the more the disease advanced, the more veins had to be added. We also created appliances for the hands and feet, to simulate the fingers and toes fusing together.

As the disease continued to progress, the characters became

Leyor of the Caldonians (Kevin Peter Hall) was Westmore's first attempt to do something elaborate with an alien forehead.

"The Price" Photo: ©1990 Paramount Pictures

Singer Mick Fleetwood played one of the fish-like Antedians in "Manhunt."

even more lizard-like. We changed the nose and muzzle area, adding an appliance to make it look like a reptilian snout, and continued to add more blue veins. There's a great shot of Maryann in Sick Bay as she's being examined by Dr. Crusher, where we get to see the makeup in its intermediate stage.

The final stage of the transformation took over six hours to apply to LeVar's head and body. He had appliances on his head, hands and feet, and his entire body was covered with tiny blue veins. He had to stand there for six hours as five makeup artists glued on the veins, which then had to be hand-painted with fluorescent paint to make them glow. We also gave him yellow contact lenses, which were treated by an eye doctor on the set. He wiped LeVar's eyes with a special stick

normally used for glaucoma testing, which makes the eyes glow when exposed to a black light.

LeVar's final lizard makeup was actually difficult to see properly, because most of those scenes were shot in darkness with a black light. There is a good shot of Geordi in the Transporter Room just before he beams down to the planet, and if you look closely, you can see him just before he disappears. There were a few other shots, which had to be cut for time reasons.

In addition to the makeups we applied on LeVar and Maryann, wardrobe also had to create two full body suits—and we built the heads, hands and feet—which were worn by Mark and Brian, two local radio personalities here in California who wanted to do the show. Since they were both too

busy for fittings, we had to make the suits in pieces that could be slipped together. On the day of filming, Mark and Brian actually conducted their radio show in our studio while they were being dressed. Even with the pre-painted suits, it still took two hours to glue everything on.

The Trill

Creating the Trill, the symbiotic species seen in "The Host," was a two-fold challenge. Not only did we have to devise a makeup concept for the humanoid hosts, but I also had to design the symbiont itself; the being that lived *inside* the host.

For the hosts, I devised a makeup consisting of an appliance for the nose and forehead to make them slightly different, but still recognizably humanoid. For

Jonathan Frakes, on being a Mintakan

"My experience with being a Mintakan gave me great appreciation for what Dorn goes through every morning," Frakes admits. "I think the makeup took something like two-and-a-half hours, but I don't sit very well; I get very fidgety. The look was astounding. You're amazed at how people react when you have it on. I'll do the occasional Mintakan, but I'm very thankful I have my own face."

"I had a lot to do with Jonathan's look, says director Cliff Bole, "which was created as a fast concept, and quickly executed by Michael.

"That was an intense makeup," says Frakes referring to the episode "First Contact." "I got plugs stuck up my nose, and various other things, but it was even more intense after being beaten up. Westmore does great beating up as you can see from Mr. DeNiro."

Carolyn Seymour, who also played a Romulan commander in "Contagion," returned as a Malcorian scientist.

the scene where Odan (played by Franc Luz) is injured in an accident, I had to build a rubber stomach area, adding hair to it so that it would blend into the actor's own torso. There were three bladders underneath the false skin, so that when his stomach had to pulsate, indicating the presence of a creature underneath, we were able to blow into a series of air tubes, which expanded the bladders. The surrounding rubber was very soft, and we were able to make the bladders swell quite a bit.

In creating the symbiont itself, I designed it with a long, thick body like a caterpillar, and added a hook on the front. The back body was based on an octopus, although I added some extra convolutions to give the impression of a large brain. There was a bladder built into the domed part of the creature to make it pulsate, and I used fluorescent paint on it that would glow when exposed to black light.

After Odan's original host body dies, the symbiont has to be transferred into Riker's body tem-

porarily, and there's a scene in Sick Bay where we had to show the creature being implanted. We built a false chest for Jonathan that could be opened during surgery, and I attached a line of monofilament to the creature's hooked head. As we were shooting the scene, I had to lay underneath the table, pulling on the line, to make it look as though the symbiont was able to crawl down

Dr. Crusher transfers the symbiont to Riker's body in "The Host."

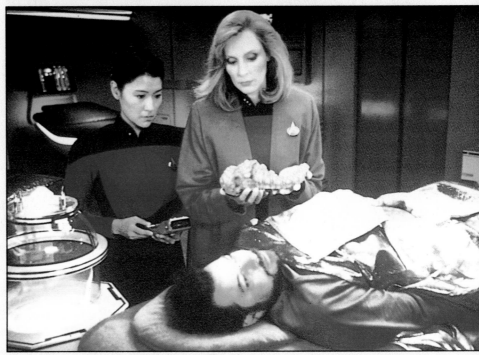

"The Host" Photo by Michael Paris: ©1991 Paramount Pictures

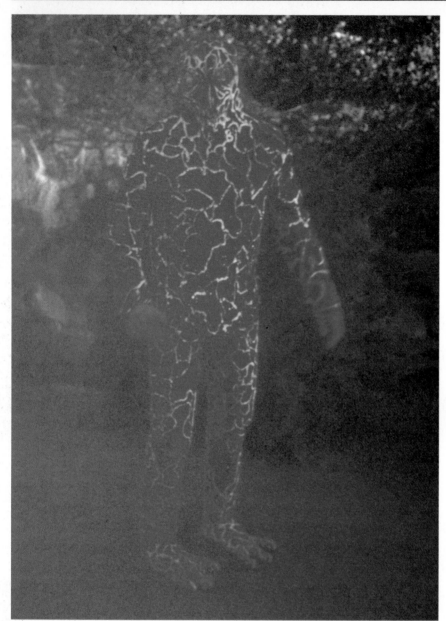

"I remember when Michael Westmore turned me into a lizard," says LeVar Burton on "Identity Crisis." "It was something like a seven-hour makeup job, while they painted all those veins on my body, which was excruciating, but you know what? It looked great!"

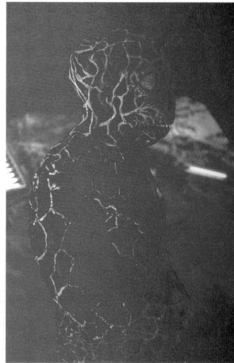

LeVar Burton had to remain standing for six hours as tiny veins were individually glued to his body in "Identity Crisis".

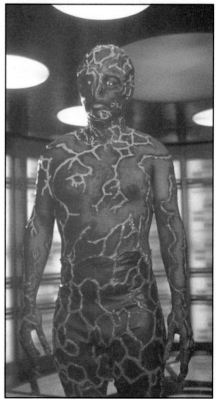

into Jonathan's body. It was all done in close-up, and looked very convincing.

The Tamarians

One of the best makeups done for the fifth season was our design for the Tamarians, featured in the story "Darmok." Since the story was about two races separated by lack of a common language, we wanted to create a race of humanoids that were similar to humans, but had major physical differences. We also knew that the Tamarian captain, played by Paul Winfield, would have a lot of screen time, and we wanted his makeup to look interesting.

As I started sculpting Paul's head, I quickly realized that I wasn't going to be adding a lot to the design in terms of size. Paul is a very big man with a large head, and adding even a thin layer of appliances to his face would still increase the overall size. I created one large piece that covered the entire head, coming down and around the eyes. There was a second piece that came across the upper lip; I made it so it could be adjusted for the different actors.

Once the makeup was applied, we airbrushed in the orange spots and patterns of the skin. These patterns were different for each of the Tamarians, although I used Paul's makeup as the basis for the

Each of the small Bajoran facial appliances is subtly different.

other actors. Their facial features, and the general shape of their heads ensured that no two characters looked exactly alike, despite their appliances.

In addition to the Tamarians, my department helped create the monster that Picard and Captain Dathon have to fight. We knew the creature was going to be optically enhanced, but it was still necessary to construct a general shape. While we built the head and hands, the costume department created the body. The final creature was gigantic; the head mold alone required almost 200 pounds of plaster and had to be made in three pieces. Because of the monster's great size, we had to build it out of polyurethane instead of the usual foam rubber, which never could have handled the stress.

For close-ups, the head was placed on a stand, with a lever that could open and close its mouth. For just a few frames of film, they shot about 30 takes of the thing twisting its head and opening its mouth.

The Bajorans

We haven't seen much of the Bajorans yet, but they promise to be an important part of our upcoming series, *DEEP SPACE NINE.* Since the Bajoran/Cardassian war is supposed to be a major element of the new show, I'm sure we'll be seeing many new Bajoran characters.

The actual Bajoran makeup is deceptively simple, and was originally created for Michelle Forbes, who plays Ensign Ro Laren. Since Michelle is an attractive woman, we wanted to come up with something that makes her look a little different than the rest of the crew, but wouldn't detract from her appearance.

I designed a small appliance that started between Michelle's eyebrows, and added a row of tiny ridges to the bridge of her nose. I made the piece very light and thin; in fact, if you threw it on a scale, it would probably weigh

Director Les Landau on Ensign Ro

"I'll tell you a funny story about the nose piece that she wears," Les Landau says. "I think they were looking for something very distinctive, yet something simple, so Michael came up with this appliance that would go on the nose, which was simple to apply yet very distinctive. During the course of shooting, Michelle Forbes and I were trying to figure out the history behind the nose, and I think I finally told her that it was an erogenous zone for Bajorans, not to be taken lightly, and not to let people mess with it. Whether or not she used it in future episodes I don't know, but it was a funny moment."

less than half a gram. I just wanted a thin skin with some detailing that would move with Michelle's own features.

We used the same type of appliances for the other Bajorans in "Ensign Ro," but I made subtle changes in it for each character. For the men, the piece was larger, and I varied the number of ridges. I think Michelle's makeup has seven ridges, while the other Bajorans might have had as few as five, or as many as nine. Even with a simple design, it's always nice to add a little variety.

The "Unification" Girls

Every once in a while, we create a makeup for THE NEXT GENERATION that, for one reason or another, doesn't get the film coverage it deserves. It's something you learn to live with, but it's sometimes frustrating to create a character you're really proud of, and it winds up getting a few seconds of screen time. That's always the makeup artist's opinion.

The two girls made up for "Unification, Part II" are a good example. There's a scene where Omag, the fat Ferengi, walks into the bar with an exotic alien woman on each arm. Each of those characters took about four hours to make up, and I know Bob Blackman spent a lot of time designing their costumes, which were absolutely gorgeous. Both characters are interesting enough to bring back, but it took so long to shoot that particular scene, there was no time to give them individual coverage. I've always considered those two makeups as particular favorites of mine.

One girl wore a small humanoid appliance between her eyes, and small upward darting eye brows. Her hairstyle was outstanding, as it formed a huge spreading fan.

The second girl was reptilian and yellow in appearance. Multicolored jewels, which were part of her costume, were also attached to the back of her protruding head. The top of her head and stomach was hand-painted and airbrushed in the design of an exotic mosquito.

Etana's (Katherine Moffat) long, glamorous fingernails kept popping off during her scene with Riker.

Instead of creating a forehead appliance for the Ullians, Westmore decided to do something for the temporal area.

The Ullians

As I started thinking about ideas for the Ullians, the race of telepathic humanoids introduced in "Violations," I wanted to do something a little different with them. Instead of creating some sort of forehead appliance, I decided to work with the temporal area at the side of the head. The makeup we created looks like a pattern of suction cups, which were bigger for the men and slightly smaller for the woman. We also added more lines and wrinkles for the older characters, suggesting that the temporal patterns change as they get older.

Once the appliances had been glued to the side of the head, we took hair and laid it over the upper edge of the pieces, so it looked as though the pattern was a normal part of the skin, and their hair would naturally grow over it. I thought it was a very subtle makeup that worked very effectively without drawing too much attention to itself.

The Satarrans

The Satarran character we created for "Conundrum" was probably one of the most time-consuming and expensive makeups we've ever done on THE NEXT GENERATION, and yet it was only seen for a few seconds.

I had to design a character that would be seen at the very end of the story, when the crew realizes that Keiran MacDuff (played by Erich Anderson) is actually an alien spy disguised as a human. When they fire their phasers at him, his skin melts away, and before it regenerates, we catch a brief look at the metallic alien hidden beneath it.

We knew ahead of time that the creature would be seen as part of an optical effect, rather than a makeup that would be applied to Erich. I worked with makeup artist Ed French, who helped me sculpt the alien's head and chest, and we worked on and off for about four days to finish it. The finished Satarran was stunning, even by the

Because the actress who played Etana had a very high forehead, I decided to create an appliance that would give her a large, bulbous forehead. We added a long red wig, like a lion's mane, to accentuate that look. I applied a total high fashion makeup, including eye makeup, false lashes, and full lips. The idea was that even though she was from another planet, Riker would still find her seductively attractive.

I also decided to give her a set of long, glamorous fingernails, and spent a long time painting and airbrushing them in hot colors. Unfortunately, we decided to glue them on with a temporary nail glue, and they kept popping off. During her scene with Riker, she spent a lot of time grabbing and chasing him around, so we had to follow her around the set, retrieving the nails and gluing them back on.

The Ktarians

When I was creating the makeup for Etana, the Ktarian woman that Riker meets in "The Game," I wanted her to look beautiful and alien at the same time; not always an easy thing.

The briefly-seen Satarran head in "Conundrum" took four days to sculpt.

The makeup for the J'naii deliberately avoided the use of cosmetics such as mascara, eyeliner or lipstick.

show's high standards.

We mounted the head and torso on a stand, and our visual effects department shot it frame-by-frame. The opticals were added into the final shot, but only a fleeting glimpse of our work was ever seen.

If we were able to redo that shot, I might have suggested that we pause a second longer so we could see more of the alien before his skin regenerated. There was a lot of nice detailing that was lost, and we even added a slight glow to the exoskeleton of the creature. I suppose we might be able to use the Satarran alien again in a future episode, because so little of it was actually seen.

The J'naii

It's not as easy as one would think to create a race of humanoids that look androgynous, and yet different from one another. That's the challenge I faced with the J'naii, the sexless species featured in "The Outcast." The way we solved the problem was to hire women of varying ages to play the parts, and then taped down their breasts to give them the same physical appearance.

In designing the makeup, I realized that the one facial feature that distinguishes men from women is the eyebrow area. Men usually have bigger, fuller eyebrows, while women tend to pluck

and shape theirs. I created a subtle forehead piece that covered the eyebrows, and then applied a light flesh tone to the entire face. We deliberately avoided the use of any highlights or shadows, as well as any other cosmetics, such

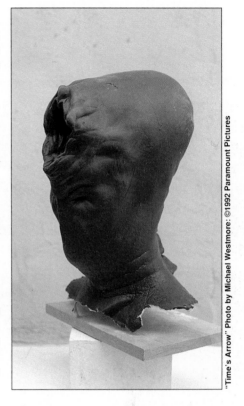

as mascara, eye liner or lipstick. The result was a race of beings that shared the same look, but were still individuals. Each character would still have their own unique set of facial features, but they all shared the same "neutered" look. It was an interesting experiment, and I think it was quite successful in satisfying the demands of the story.

"Time's Arrow" Aliens

In the final episode of Season Five, the script called for a tall, sightless alien with no facial features that could absorb energy through an opening in the forehead. The heads were not easy to maneuver in, because of limited vision through pinholes, and breathing tubes which extended out the back of the head.

The entire head and body suits were painted with chroma-key blue paint, so visual effects could create a ghost-like image. ●

Captain Dathon: Step-by-Step

In this step-by-step series, Westmore transforms Paul Winfield into a Tamarian. After applying the facial pieces, the orange spots and skin patterns were individually airbrushed. Right: Paul Winfield as Captain Dathon was one of the best makeups done for the fifth season.

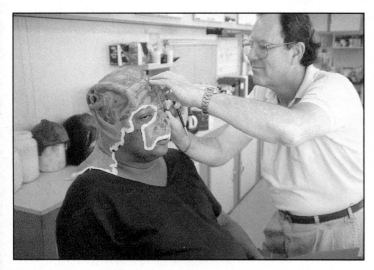

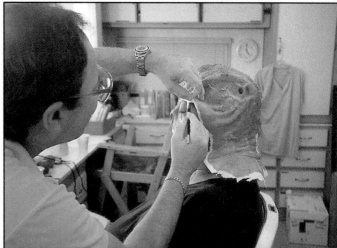

"Darmok" Photo by Robbie Robinson: ©1992 Paramount Pictures

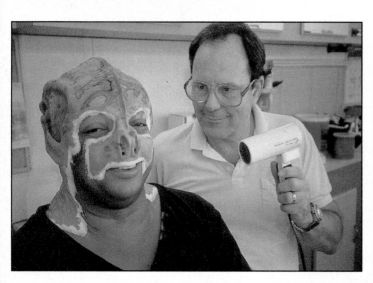

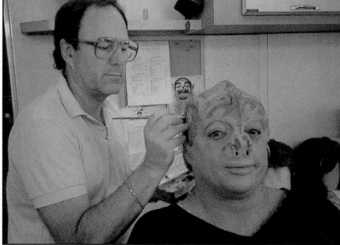

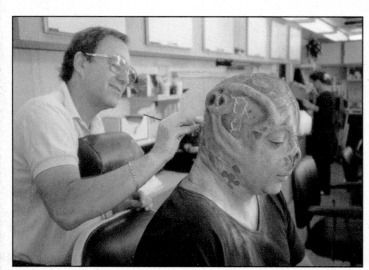

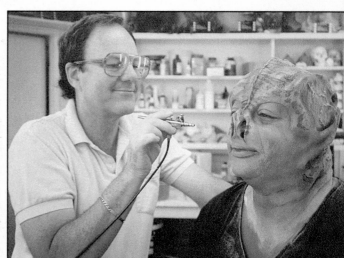

The Future

Michael Westmore

As we begin work on the sixth season of *STAR TREK: THE NEXT GENERATION*, it appears that I'll be spending the next several years going where no makeup artist has gone before. Although it's still too early to tell, there's a good chance the series may run beyond season six. There are still a lot of new worlds and new civilization to explore, and I'm glad to be a part of it.

Then there's *DEEP SPACE NINE*. As of this writing, we're all busy at work on the *STAR TREK* spinoff series, which promises to be just as exciting as *THE NEXT GENERATION*. I'm already starting to think about some of the new characters that we'll be introducing, as well as re-designing a few old favorites, who will be crossing over into the new series.

Of course, there's always the possibility of a *NEXT GENERATION* feature film. It seems inevitable when the series finally ends, whether it's one year from now or three, that a feature will be made.

It's a little strange to think that I may still be working on *STAR TREK*, in one form or another through the year 2000, but it seems strangely appropriate. As we get ready to enter the 21st Century, I can't think of another universe where I'd rather be.

Joe Nazzaro

Joe Nazzaro, a New Jersey-based writer/interviewer, has been covering science-fiction television for several years. Some of the programs that he has covered include *Doctor Who, Blake's 7, Red Dwarf,* and of course, *STAR TREK: THE NEXT GENERATION. The Makeup FX Journal* began as an interview with Michael Westmore, and grew into an in-depth account of the program's makeup effects. Nazzaro hopes to do a follow-up volume in the near future.

"One of the most exciting aspects of working on *THE NEXT GENERATION* is having to come up with complicated makeup effects within a relatively short period of time."

—Michael Westmore